240

BRINGING THE MASS TO THE PEOPLE

Sacrae memoriae Pii XII[i] Papae
instauratori sacrae liturgiae

Bringing the Mass to the People

BY THE REVEREND H. A. REINHOLD

with an Introduction by Frederick R. McManus, J.C.D.

HELICON PRESS · BALTIMORE 27, MARYLAND

Nihil obstat: JACOB C. SHINAR, J.C.L.
Censor deputatus

Imprimatur: ✠ JOHN J. WRIGHT, D.D.
Bishop of Pittsburgh
May 31, 1960

The *Nihil obstat* and *Imprimatur* are official declarations that a book or pamphlet is free of doctrinal or moral error. No implication is contained therein that those who have granted the *Nihil obstat* and *Imprimatur* agree with the opinions expressed.

PRINTED IN THE UNITED STATES OF AMERICA BY THE NORTH CENTRAL PUBLISHING COMPANY, ST. PAUL, MINNESOTA

Acknowledgments

This book would never have been written had it not been for the leisure afforded by a prolonged convalescence. That I should find myself here in Pittsburgh, I owe to the generosity of Bishop John J. Wright, whose hospitality has made it possible for me to serve the Liturgical Movement with the pen, just as in the preceding years I have enjoyed the generous hospitality of the Cardinal Archbishops of Boston and New York and my loyal friends, Monsignor Edward G. Murray and Father E. Harold Smith. With their help and encouragement during these four long years I have gradually returned to better health. To all these, I offer this small book as a token of gratitude.

To Father Frederick R. McManus, J.C.D., of the Catholic University of America, I am deeply indebted for his Introduction and his many valuable suggestions and corrections, as also to Mrs. Mary Perkins Ryan for editorial assistance, and to Mrs. Elizabeth Williams Jesukiewicz for the typing of the final version.

I am grateful to Sheed and Ward for permission to use the Knox translation of the Bible, and to Dom Murray and the editors of *The Furrow* for permission to use Dom Murray's translation of the Canon.

Needless to say, I feel a profound debt of gratitude to all the scholars and pastors on whose labors this report is based, above all to those whose ideas and suggestions I have incorporated in this book. Their names will be found in the text and footnotes.

H. A. REINHOLD

Pittsburgh, Pa.
Third Sunday after Easter, 1960

Contents

BRINGING THE MASS TO THE PEOPLE

Introduction

"A long period of years must pass before the liturgical edifice, which the mystical Spouse of Christ has formed in her zeal and understanding to proclaim her piety and faith, may again appear splendid with dignity and harmony, as cleansed of the accumulations of age." These words, referring to the needed restoration of the Roman rite, are not the rabid complaining of a discontented reformer, but the solemn judgment of Pope St. Pius X.[1]

The word chosen by the supreme pontiff to describe the condition of the liturgical rites in 1913 was "squalor," which means the roughness arising from dirt and neglect, filthiness. This is a harsh saying, but it does suggest the need for constant emendation and development of the sacred liturgy; it may not be "neglected." This was recognized by the Council of Trent when it commanded that the reform of the Missal and Breviary should be handed over to the Roman pontiff;[2] by Pope Sixtus V, when he entrusted the "reform and correction of the liturgical books" to the new Congregation of Sacred Rites and Ceremonies in 1588;[3] by Pope Pius XI, when in 1930 he established a historical section of the same congregation to provide, among

[1] Pius X, motu proprio, *Abhinc duos annos* (October 23, 1913), AAS, 5 (1913), 449–450.
[2] Continuation of Session XXV, *de indice Librorum et Catechismo, Breviario et Missali*, December 4, 1563.
[3] Bull, *Immensa aeterni Dei* (January 22, 1588), *Bullarum Diplomatum et Privilegiorum Romanorum Pontificum Taurinensis Editio* (Turin, 1857–1872), VIII, 989–990.

3

other things, the historical study necessary for reforming, correcting and publishing new editions of the liturgical books.[4]

In the midst of the most considerable liturgical reform in four centuries, the late Holy Father, Pius XII, explained the objective need for such emendation of sacred rites:

> The ecclesiastical hierarchy . . . has not hesitated — keeping the substance of the eucharistic sacrifice of the altar and of the sacraments carefully intact — to change anything which it did not consider entirely fitting, and to add what seemed more suitable for the increase of honor to Jesus Christ and the august Trinity, and for the instruction and salutary stimulation of the Christian people."[5]

These words of the Roman pontiff should be sufficient justification for this book, since they are a clear recognition that the accepted liturgical forms are sometimes imperfect. The widespread failure to accept this necessarily changeable character of the sacred liturgy makes the book a necessity.

Nevertheless an appreciation of what is meant by liturgy must precede any proper understanding of its vital growth or progress. Ordinarily it would be unwise to approach the definition of such a thing as liturgy negatively, but for this we may again call upon the teaching of the late pontiff. In offering what will doubtless be an enduring doctrine on the liturgy's true meaning, Pius XII was just as insistent on what the liturgy is not.

1. Catholic public worship is not merely external. To assert this would be the gravest of errors. The liturgy is both internal and external and it is the inner element which is primary. In

---

[4] Motu proprio, *Già da qualche tempo* (February 6, 1930), AAS, 22 (1930), 87–88.

[5] Encyclical letter, *Mediator Dei* (November 20, 1947) [§ 49], AAS, 39 (1947), 541. (The references to the sections of this encyclical, given in brackets, are not from the original text in AAS, but are inserted in the various translations for the sake of convenience.)

On another occasion, the Holy Father declared: "There are found in the liturgy unchangeable elements, a sacred content which transcends time, but also elements which are variable and transitory, and sometimes even imperfect" (Allocution of September 22, 1956, AAS, 48 [1956], 723–724, and *The Assisi Papers* [Collegeville, Minn.: The Liturgical Press, 1957], p. 235).

every case the outward manifestation of worship — made necessary by the social character of liturgy — is the expression of inner faith and devotion, which are truly liturgical acts.[6]

2. The offerer of the liturgy is not the priest alone, nor the baptized faithful in union with the priest alone, nor even Christ Jesus alone. The doer of the act of liturgy is the whole Christ: Head and members.

Christ is the principal Liturgist, the high priest of the New Law. The baptized, the confirmed, the ordained Christian share, in different ways, in that priesthood. With Christ and in Christ and through Christ the Church offers the liturgy of prayer, praise and sacrifice. And Christ Himself is present at every liturgical act: the eucharistic sacrifice, the celebration of the sacraments, and the ecclesiastical prayer.[7]

3. The liturgy does not consist of human elements alone. The liturgy is not something added by ecclesiastical authority to things of divine institution. Thus, it is erroneous to contrast the "Mass" (thought of as the essential acts determined by Christ's will) with the "liturgy" (thought of as some prayers and rites added by the Church). Both are, in the teaching of Pius XII, "liturgy." The worship of God offered by Christ and His Church includes both elements, divine and human.[8]

Put another way, this means that the liturgy *is* the Mass, the sacraments, the Church's prayer. With a keen sense of its deepest meaning, the Oriental Churches have reserved the word *liturgia* (public religious service) for the eucharistic Sacrifice; for them there can be no confusion concerning the meaning of the liturgy which is offered by the Lord to the Father.

4. Finally, the sacred liturgy should not be confused with

[6] *Mediator Dei* [§§ 23–25], *loc. cit.*, pp. 530–532.
[7] *Ibid.* [§ 20], *loc. cit.*, pp. 528–529.
[8] *Ibid.* [§ 50], *loc. cit.*, pp. 541–542. In this connection it is interesting to compare the definition of public worship in canon 1256 with the Instruction of September 3, 1958, issued by the Congregation of Rites (AAS, 50 [1958], 630–663). This canon speaks only of acts instituted by the Church as pertaining to public cult (*per actus ex Ecclesiae institutione*); the Instruction, defining "liturgical *actiones*" in § 1, speaks of actions "instituted by Jesus Christ or the Church" (*ex institutione Iesu Christi vel Ecclesiae*). In other words, the liturgy embraces both the rites instituted by Christ and the rites instituted by the Church.

the rubrics or laws which guide and govern it. The inner prayer should conform to the outward word and it is the law which determines what words (and acts) are part of the sacred liturgy. But this is not to say that liturgy is a body of rules or regulations issued by authority — the laws only place the words on our lips, and the words must be filled with prayer and praise.[9]

These rather negative considerations — of what the liturgy is *not* — are needed so long as some persist in regarding the papal liturgical revival as esoteric or external or rubrical, so long as the public worship of the Church is not the chief source of Christian piety and faith as well as the cult due to God almighty.[10] The positive and eminently satisfactory definition of the liturgy is that given by Pius XII in the encyclical letter *Mediator Dei*:

> The sacred liturgy is the public worship which our Redeemer as Head of the Church renders to the heavenly Father, and which the community of the faithful of Christ renders to its Founder and through Him to the eternal Father. It is, in brief, the integral, public worship of the Mystical Body of Jesus Christ, namely, of the Head and His members.[11]

A significant explanation of the phrase "integral public worship" has been offered by Abbot Bernard Capelle:

> It is integral because it belongs to Christ and the Church inseparably; it is integral also because it includes the sacraments as well as prayer and sacrifice; it [is integral because it] includes the annual cycle of the mysteries of

[9] Cf. *Mediator Dei* [§ 25], *loc. cit.*, p. 532.
[10] Pius X, motu proprio, *Inter pastoralis officii sollicitudines* (November 22, 1903), ASS, 41 (1903–1904), 387–395; Pius XI, encyclical letter, *Quas primas* (December 11, 1925), AAS, 17 (1925), 603; audience with B. Capelle (December 3, 1935), *Les Questions liturgiques et paroissiales,* 21 (1936), 4; Bugnini, *Documenta Pontificia ad Instaurationem Liturgicam Spectantia* (1903–1953) (Rome: Edizioni Liturgiche, 1953), pp. 70–71; Pius XII, Allocution of September 22, 1956, AAS, 48 (1956), 723–724; *The Assisi Papers,* p. 225.
[11] *Loc. cit.*, pp. 528–529.

Christ, as well as the sanctoral cycle interwoven with it.[12]

This explanation enforces the point already made: that the doer of the liturgy of the New Law is the whole Christ, the Head and His members. It indicates, moreover, the material scope or content of the holy liturgy: the Mass, the sacraments and sacramentals, and the Church's prayer — celebrated throughout a liturgical year dedicated to the Christian mystery in all its saving aspects.

The same explanation, now in the form of a canonical definition, was given by the Congregation of Sacred Rites in the instruction issued by authority of Pius XII on September 3, 1958:

> Liturgical *actiones* are those sacred actions, which, instituted by Jesus Christ or the Church and in their name, are carried out in accordance with the liturgical books approved by the Holy See by persons legitimately deputed, to give due worship to God, the saints, or the blessed . . .[13]

This principle, which in the strict sense has binding-force throughout the Latin Church,[14] has its greatest utility as a working norm. The Apostolic See sets and determines the scope of the liturgy through the approbation it gives to the official liturgical books of each rite. For the Roman rite the chief liturgical

---

[12] "The Pastoral Theology of the Encyclicals *Mystici Corporis* and *Mediator Dei*," *The Assisi Papers*, p. 35.

[13] § 1, AAS, 50 (1958), 630–663.

[14] *Ibid.* § 11, *loc. cit.*, p. 634. This means in effect that the several non-Roman rites of the Latin Church are affected by this definition (as well as by the entire Instruction of S.R.C. of September 3, 1958). This would include the Ambrosian or Milanese rite, the Mozarabic or Toledan rite, the rites of Braga and Lyons, as well as the rites of the religious orders: Carthusian, Cistercian, Premonstratensian, Carmelite and Dominican. From a slightly different viewpoint, the so-called "Glagolitic" rite is included; this is the Roman rite, but it is celebrated in the Slavonic language, according to its own liturgical books.

Canon 1257 reserves to the Holy See the right to approve the liturgical books of the Latin Church. A similar provision with regard to the liturgical books of the Oriental Churches is found in canon 279, § 2 of the motu proprio *Cleri sanctitati* of Pius XII (June 2, 1957), AAS, 49 (1957), 518.

books are of course the Roman Missal (for the holy Sacrifice), the Roman Pontifical and Ritual (for sacraments and sacramentals), and the Roman Breviary (for the divine Office).[15] The public worship of Christ and His Church thus embraces the Eucharist, sacrifice and sacrament, the other sacraments and sacramentals related to the Eucharist, as well as the prayer by which the hours, days, and years are made holy to the Lord.

Our purpose is to look beyond the holy liturgy as it is found in the liturgical books and celebrated in our times. We must at

[15] The following are the general liturgical books of the Roman rite, as enumerated by the Holy See (S.R.C., decree of August 10, 1946, AAS, 38 [1946], 371–372):
Breviarium Romanum
Missale Romanum (now including the *Ordo Hebdomadae Sanctae Instauratus*, the former text of the Missal for Holy Week having been suppressed — S.R.C. decree, *Maxima redemptionis nostrae mysteria* [November 16, 1955], AAS, 47 [1955], 838–841).
Rituale Romanum
Pontificale Romanum
Caeremoniale Episcoporum (norms for the pontifical celebration of sacred rites. Chapters 21–28 of book II have been suppressed and replaced by *Ritus Pontificalis Ordinis Hebdomadae Sanctae Instaurati* — S.R.C. decree, *Ut sacri ritus* [February 15, 1957]).
Memoriale Rituum (for use in smaller churches on certain occasions. Chapters III–VI have been suppressed and replaced by *Ritus Simplex Ordinis Hebdomadae Sanctae Instaurati* — S.R.C. decree, *Edito Ordine* [February 5, 1957]).
Octavarium Romanum (a book of lessons for use during octaves. This has been made obsolete by the decree on the simplification of the rubrics — S.R.C. [March 23, 1955], II, 11; AAS, 47 [1955], 218–224).
Decreta Authentica Congregationis Sacrorum Rituum (the collected decrees of the Congregation of Rites. These include, among other things, the *Instructio Clementina*, on the Forty Hours' Devotion).
To these must be added the following liturgical books of chant (S.R.C. instruction, *De musica sacra et sacra liturgia* [September 3, 1958], § 56, AAS, 50 [1958], 648–649):
Graduale Romanum with the *Ordinarium Missae* (corresponding to the Roman Missal).
Antiphonale Romanum for the day hours (corresponding to the Roman Breviary, but lacking the hour of Matins).
Officium Defunctorum, Maioris hebdomadae and *Nativitatis D. N. Iesu Christi* (the complete sung office of the Dead and for Holy Week and Christmas).
In addition there are numerous "particular" liturgical books approved by the Holy See for individual dioceses, for the dioceses of a given country or region or for religious institutes. These may be the propers for certain feasts or such volumes as the bilingual rituals, in the form of appendices to the Roman Ritual, etc.
The other rites of the Latin Church have similar liturgical books, although these are usually not so numerous or complete. It is often necessary for such rites to use a Roman liturgical book, such as the Pontifical, in defect of a proper book.

least suggest how the liturgical rites are formed and, in the present context, changed.

At the beginning of the twentieth century, St. Pius X took the first — limited but significant — step toward a liturgical restoration.[16] After a lapse, this was taken up again by Pope Pius XII with the establishment, on May 28, 1948, of a pontifical commission for the general restoration of the liturgy.[17] A few months earlier, however, the late Holy Father had explained how public worship should develop and does develop:

> The sacred liturgy includes divine as well as human elements. The former, as is clear, cannot be changed in any way by men, since they were instituted by the Divine Redeemer. But the latter admit of various modifications as the needs of the age, circumstances, and men require and which the ecclesiastical hierarchy under the guidance of the Holy Spirit approves.
>
> Thus has arisen the marvelous variety of Eastern and Western rites, thus the gradual growth occurs by which are evolved, step by step, particular customs of religious worship and particular works of piety, only slightly discernible in earlier ages. Thus it happens from time to time that pious practices, lost in the course of time, are again called into use, and again renewed.
>
> All these developments testify to the life of the immaculate Spouse of Jesus Christ, vigorous through these

[16] "But, since the arrangement of the Psalter [reformed in 1911] has an intimate connection with the entirety of the divine Office and the liturgy, it is clear to all that through what is here decreed we have taken the first step toward the emendation of the Roman Breviary and Missal . . ." (Pius X, bull, *Divino afflatu* [November 1, 1911]).

[17] *Ephemerides liturgicae*, 72 (1958), 377. The principal achievements of the Commission up to the present are the restoration of the Easter Vigil (1951) and of Holy Week (1955), the provisional simplification of the rubrics of the Breviary and — to a lesser degree — the Missal (1955), and the Instruction on sacred music and the liturgy formulated by the Commission with the cooperation of experts on sacred music (1958). The body has been referred to in pontifical documents as the "particular commission of experts to whom the study of the general liturgical restoration has been entrusted" (S.R.C. decr. gen., *Cum nostra hac aetate* [March 23, 1955], AAS, 46 [1955], 218), and more simply as the "Pontifical Commission for the general liturgical restoration" (S.R.C. Instruction of September 3, 1958, AAS, 50 [1958], 631).

many centuries. They express the sacred language which has passed between her and her divine Spouse as the ages run their course, to profess her own faith, with that of the nations entrusted to her care, and her own unfailing love. They prove, likewise, the wisdom of her teaching method, by which each day she arouses and nourishes the "Christian instinct" in those who believe.[18]

From this authoritative explanation, several points may be made, each of great significance:

1. The human elements in the liturgy may be modified.

2. While such modifications are due to the needs of the faithful in the changing circumstances of the times, the ultimate determination of the changes rests with the ecclesiastical authority.

3. Changes in the liturgy are a positive good and are evidence of the Church's vitality.

The purpose of liturgical development is twofold, as expounded by Pius XII in a passage already quoted: "the increase of honor to Jesus Christ and the august Trinity" and "the instruction and salutary stimulation of the Christian people." [19] Let the order be noted: Important as the instruction and edification of the faithful are, the primary purpose of liturgy is worship. Therefore, liturgical reform should first strive for the worship of God in a way that is objectively more suitable, objectively more worthy of our concept of the Creator's transcendent majesty.

It is possible to point out many causes and occasions which have — in the long history of liturgical development — contributed to the present liturgy. Again, Pius XII provides an enumeration of such causes: clearer formulation of doctrine, changes in the discipline of the sacraments, the contribution of popular devotions and nonliturgical practices of piety, the progress in the arts which serve liturgical worship.[20] To these must

[18] *Mediator Dei* [§ 50], *loc. cit.*, pp. 541–542.
[19] *Ibid.* [§ 49], *loc. cit.*, p. 541.
[20] *Ibid.* [§§ 52–56], *loc. cit.*, pp. 542–543.

be added, in the present context of liturgical reform, a balanced and conscious attempt to restore the legitimate traditions of the Roman rite and to serve the spiritual needs of the flock in the twentieth century.[21]

A single example may illustrate this. It shows both of the purposes at work and the rather slow and gradual action of the Holy See in these matters. At the beginning of the twentieth century the Lenten liturgy — one of the glories of the Roman rite — had deteriorated gravely. So many saints' feasts had intruded on the season that the Lenten weekday Mass-formularies were largely neglected.

The situation was partially remedied by St. Pius X who permitted, at the option of the celebrating priest, the celebration of the Lenten Mass in place of the Mass of most saints' days.[22] At once this action served as a partial restoration of the traditional liturgy (whereby the Roman rite provided a complete set of Mass-formularies for the Lenten weekdays) and as a stimulus to popular appreciation and edification (through the long neglected prayers, psalms, and lessons of the same Mass texts).

The next step had to wait forty years. In 1955 Pope Pius XII extended the principle further and allowed the recitation of the Lenten weekday office of prayer to replace, optionally again, the saints' feast-day office during the Lenten season.[23] What may be predicted for the future? Most likely the removal from Lent of the feasts of the saints — not to diminish the honor shown them but to fortify the Lenten piety of the faithful in accordance with the history of the Roman rite.[24]

To mention only the action taken by the Apostolic See is to treat the finished product, as it were, taking no account of the

[21] Cf. F. Antonelli, "The Liturgical Reform of Holy Week: Importance, Realizations, Perspectives," *The Assisi Papers*, pp. 152–153.
[22] Pius X, motu proprio, *Abhinc duos annos* (October 23, 1913), AAS, 5 (1913), 449–450.
[23] S.R.C. general decree, *Cum nostra hac aetate* (March 23, 1955), AAS, 46 (1955), 218.
[24] G. Card. Lercaro, "The Simplification of the Rubrics and the Breviary Reform," *The Assisi Papers*, p. 207; cf. A. Bugnini, *Commentarium ad Decretum S.R.C. diei 23 Martii 1955* (Rome: Edizione Liturgiche, 1955), pp. 33–34.

preparation which such reform or restoration entails. It is obvious enough that the completion of an emended liturgical book or section of such a book requires great study both of the needs of the age and of the lawful traditions of the holy liturgy — especially when both have been overlooked for a long period.

The existence of a pontifical commission for the general restoration of the liturgy, the establishment of the historical section of the Congregation of Rites, and the consultation by the Holy See with scholars and experts [25] all help to show the picture of liturgical development at work. It does not answer fully, however, the question, How does the liturgical development take place?

It would be possible of course to indicate how in the past the liturgical forms achieved acceptance through custom and through the legislation of bishops and councils without the direct intervention of the Roman pontiff. More to the point, for the liturgical changes now taking place, are the influences which move the Holy See. These were mentioned in the decree on the restored rite of Holy Week,[26] the first great change in the Roman Missal since 1570.

After referring to the sorry condition of the liturgical observance of Holy Week, the decree continues:

> For these reasons experts in liturgical matters, priests exercising the cure of souls, and above all their Excellencies the Bishops, have in recent years presented petitions to the Holy See, asking that the liturgical services of the sacred Triduum be returned to the hours after noon, as was once done, with the purpose that all the faithful might be present more easily at these rites.[27]

This pontifical document recognizes three important sources

[25] Thus, in the preparation of the Instruction on Sacred Music and the Sacred Liturgy — more a work of codification than of reform, but certainly containing elements of the latter — experts in the field of sacred music cooperated, as the document itself indicates, cf. AAS, 50 (1958), 631.
[26] S.R.C. decree, *Maxima redemptionis nostrae mysteria* (November 16, 1955), AAS, 47 (1955), 839.
[27] *Ibid.*

of petitions for liturgical restoration addressed to the Holy See: 1) liturgical experts or scholars; 2) pastors of souls; 3) and, most important of all, the bishops. Each of these, in his concern for liturgical growth, may stress one or other aspect: the pastor principally concerned with current pastoral needs or trends, the scholar anxious to establish historical precedents as a foundation for future change. Yet ideally all should be aware in some measure of the many complex factors in ritual development; this book is a contribution to that awareness.

The part of the bishops in this is clear enough, whether they act singly or by provinces or by countries when they offer suggestions and petitions to the supreme pontiff. If such a petition is to be presented *nomine Ecclesiae*, in the name of the Church or diocese, only the bishop may present it. The requests of others must be unofficial or private. And it is evident that the requests of the bishops will receive the readiest hearing from the Apostolic See.

On the other hand, it would be a mistake to underestimate the suggestions made by others, "experts in liturgical matters" and "priests exercising the cure of souls," according to the Holy Week decree. Study, research, discussion, controversy — all play their part in the progress of the liturgy. Scientific journals, clerical magazines, learned and popular books record the experience of pastors and the debates of scholars.

Speaking to an audience of such pastors and students, the Cardinal Prefect of the Congregation of Sacred Rites expressed the desire of the Holy See for unofficial study, discussions and proposals:

> In the present congress [28] there will not be debates properly so called, but not because they might turn out to be boring or disagreeable; on the contrary, if they are properly directed and animated by the desire for good, they bring light and are the way toward equitable solutions of the problems presented. Debates are not per-

[28] The First International Congress of Pastoral Liturgy, held at Assisi and Rome, September 18–22, 1956.

mitted by the very character of this congress, which is eminently hierarchical . . . this does not exclude the possibility that various committees, on the occasion of this assembly, may take under examination various problems connected with the sacred liturgy; and such private and unofficial discussions may well result in orders of the day or in conclusions to be submitted to the ecclesiastical authority, which in its own office will take them under examination according to their merit. Looking over the documents which integrate this liturgical period, we have been able to notice that His Holiness [Pope Pius XII] welcomes with delicate courtesy what the students of the liturgy present or indicate; but in virtue of the supreme power which belongs only to him, it is the pope who fixes the principles . . .[29]

On the occasion of a congress or convention, such as the one addressed by Cardinal Cicognani, it is only to be expected that proposals or resolutions will be submitted to the ecclesiastical authority. The most notable scholarly gathering of this kind in recent years was at Lugano in 1953.[30]

Recommendations made at a congress have of course an organized character, however private and unofficial. Of equal importance are the studies and proposals of individual scholars and writers. These have been in the background of every liturgical development of the century; they are certain to be the guideposts to future development.

This is the category into which the present book fits. It is a summary or a report of proposals of experts, pastors and bishops. These have been analyzed and explained so that a truly original contribution results, since the author brings to his study years of devoted pastoral experience and the widest reading and

[29] G. Card. Cicognani, "Opening Address," *The Assisi Papers*, p. 7.
[30] Third International Congress of Liturgical Studies, September 12–18, 1953. The conclusions of this congress, together with the two which preceded it (Maria Laach, 1951 and Ste Odile, 1952) may be found in *Worship*, 27 (1954), 157–167. Similar meetings have been held in subsequent years; many of the recommendations have already been acted upon by the Holy See.

study. The proposals discussed here all have to do with the ritual aspects of the Mass. Other liturgical matters, such as vesture, language or even music, are actually beyond the scope of this book and, though they are important in themselves, may even be regarded as relatively peripheral in the discussion of so central a theme.

Much that is proposed in these pages will doubtless be found in future liturgical books, in one form or another, after it has been considered — together with a multitude of other recommendations — by the competent authority in the Church. Much may never come to pass, but this is not the issue; the issue is that out of countless studies and examinations of sources, out of practice and reflection, comes the understanding of liturgical forms without which liturgical sincerity and vitality would be impossible.

It is not necessary that we agree with all the points covered or reported by the author of this book, although most of them have every likelihood of serious consideration by the Holy See. There is the very greatest utility in the discussion itself and in the wider awareness of the matters involved.

Sometimes the repetition by the Holy See of grave warnings against certain excesses among promoters of the liturgical revival has led some to ignore the general evaluation of the liturgical movement made by the Holy See. In the same allocution in which he spoke of the movement as "a sign of the providential dispositions of God for the present time, of the movement of the Holy Ghost in the Church, to draw men more closely to the mysteries of the faith and the riches of grace which flow from the active participation of the faithful in the liturgical life," [31] Pius XII gave the following considered opinion:

> In the matter of liturgy, as in many other spheres, one must avoid two extreme attitudes with regard to the past: a blind attachment and a complete contempt. There are found in the liturgy unchangeable elements,

[31] Allocution of September 22, 1956, AAS, 48 (1956), 723–724; *The Assisi Papers*, p. 235.

a sacred content which transcends time, but also elements which are variable and transitory, and sometimes even imperfect. The present-day attitude of liturgical milieux toward the past seems to Us in general to be entirely sound . . .[32]

This balance is nowhere more evident than in works such as the present one, where pastoral concerns and the traditions of the Roman rite are carefully harmonized and where all the proposals are simply proposals reported and submitted for study and discussion, and ultimately subjected entirely to the judgment of the ecclesiastical authority.

It is unnecessary that we agree with all the proposals here assembled and codified for such study to achieve its purpose. The flowering of liturgical studies should in fact give rise to different opinions, expressed with charity and patience, based upon sound scholarship and zeal for the Kingdom of God. Even if, as seems most unlikely, very few of the restorations described here come to pass, the very discussion of them throws new lights on the shape of the Roman liturgy — long obscured by the silent Canon and by ignorance of the Latin language used in the liturgical functions of the Roman rite.

In this connection, it should be noted that the author of this book has prescinded entirely from the vernacular controversy. Fortunately, it is possible to discuss thoroughly the ritual and prayer-texts of the Roman Mass in the context of restoration, while saving for another occasion a report on the deep-seated problem of liturgical language. This the author has done, so that his study of proposed changes in the Mass of the Roman rite should not be obscured by the heated feelings, on both sides, concerning the distinct matter of the several mother tongues in the sacred liturgy.

Study and discussion, books and articles are only part of the contribution to be made by bishops, pastors, and students to the pontifical restoration of the sacred liturgy. A

[32] *Ibid.*

wide and significant place must be acknowledged for pastoral experimentation.

This is not the place to discuss the historical development of the liturgy through custom and usage and popular practice. As already mentioned, Pius XII acknowledged this as one of the occasions of liturgical change.[33] A clear example of this is the introduction of that popular or private devotional exercise called the renewal of baptismal promises into the Roman Missal.[34] What had been in existence by private authority and certainly laudable as such was after a period of practice and experiment added to the Paschal Vigil — and with its rite in the vernacular languages.[35]

Let it be said at the outset that no unauthorized experimentation with the approved liturgical books is contemplated or permissible. Neither bishop nor priest has any right to alter the Missal, the Breviary, the Ritual, whether in their printed forms or in the actual use of the texts in the course of sacred rites.[36]

The Holy See, however, has already given indications that experimentation — under its control — is an extremely useful step in the emendation of liturgical forms. With regard to the norms for the evening Mass and the eucharistic fast, a long period of experiment was employed, first through indults addressed to individuals or groups,[37] later through the appearance of an apostolic constitution[38] and its subsequent modification.[39] An even clearer example is the restoration of the Paschal Vigil, which in the first place was declared to be an experiment; and the bishops were directed to report on the success of the vigil rite.[40]

[33] *Mediator Dei* [§ 54–55], *loc. cit.*, p. 543.
[34] S.R.C. decree, *Maxima redemptionis nostrae mysteria* (November 16, 1955), AAS, 47 (1955), 838–841; Instruction, same date, *ibid.*, p. 844.
[35] *Missale Romanum*, "De vigilia paschali," no. 26.
[36] Can. 1257; S.R.C., Instruction of September 3, 1958, § 12, AAS, 50 (1958), 635–636.
[37] Pius XII, *Christus Dominus* (January 6, 1953), AAS, 45 (1953), 15–24
[38] *Ibid.*
[39] Pius XII, motu proprio, *Sacram Communionem* (March 19, 1957), AAS, 49 (1957), 177–178.
[40] S.R.C. decree, *Dominicae Resurrectionis vigiliam* (February 9, 1951),

An important means whereby the Holy See can experiment in the field of liturgical development — now that all are conscious of the possibilities of change — is through the concession of special grants to dioceses or countries. Sometimes this is at the instance of individual bishops or of the bishops of a province or of a country, less regularly through an offer of such grants by the Holy See.[41]

Today, or in recent times, indults from the Holy See allow, for example, in certain places: [42] that the vernacular languages be used in the administration of several of the sacraments, some texts being excepted; [43] that solemn Mass be celebrated without the assistance of a subdeacon — the *Missa cum diacono*;[44] that the Paschal Vigil be celebrated in the early morning hours of Easter Sunday, before dawn; that the Leonine prayers be omitted after all Masses at which a homily is given; that the Gospels of the Passion and the Lessons at the Paschal Vigil be in the vernacular, the Latin text being omitted; that the deacon, subdeacon, and lector at solemn Mass (or the celebrant and

---

AAS, 43 (1951), 128–129: "Sanctitas Sua Rubricas . . . approbare dignatus est, pro nocturna vigiliae paschalis celebratione, facultative pro hoc anno de locorum Ordinariorum prudenti iudicio instauranda, et ad experimentum. Rogantur propterea iidem locorum Ordinarii, qui hac facultate usi fuerint, ut de fidelium concursu et pietate, deque successu instauratae vigiliae paschalis S. Rituum Congregationem certiorem facere velint." The one year's experiment was continued in 1952 with an extension of three years (S.R.C. decree, *Instaurata vigilia paschalis* [January 11, 1952], AAS, 44 [1952], 48–49), then extended to the year 1955 (S.R.C. decree, *Instauratae Vigiliae Paschalis celebratio* [January 15, 1955], AAS, 47 [1955], 48). This rite, together with the entire restoration of Holy Week, was definitively inserted in the Roman Missal in November, 1955 (cf. *supra*, note 34).

[41] It has been reported that the indult to celebrate the Paschal Vigil before dawn on Easter Sunday morning mentioned below was offered to the bishops of the individual dioceses of Germany.

[42] Several of these examples are taken from mission countries. On the need for specific petitions from the individual bishops or from the bishops of a province or country, the vice-relator of the historical section of S.R.C. has stated emphatically: "The bishops must make requests, make requests, make requests." Cf. Hofinger et al., *Worship: the Life of the Missions* (Notre Dame, Indiana: University of Notre Dame Press, 1958), p. 299.

[43] As is well known, this has been widely conceded. In at least one instance (that of mission countries) the Holy See took the initiative, asking the bishops to prepare bilingual rituals, to use them for a period of ten years, and then to submit them to the Holy See for final approval; cf. Bugnini, *Documenta Pontificia*, pp. 173–174.

[44] This is already permitted throughout the Roman rite during Holy Week; cf. S.R.C., *ordinationes et declarationes* (February 1, 1957), AAS, 49 (1957), 91–5.

lector at *Missa Cantata*) recite the vernacular Scripture Lesson proper to each immediately after the chanting of the Latin text;[45] that at sung parochial Masses the congregation may chant the Kyrie, Gloria, Creed, Sanctus and Agnus Dei in the vernacular language — in the case of the Gloria and Creed, after the Latin intonation by the celebrant; that blessings of the Roman Ritual be translated and recited in the vernacular, in a version to be approved by the bishops; that a proper preface for Advent and for Corpus Christi be sung or recited at Mass;[46] that the Greater and Lesser Litanies be celebrated at a period of the year suitable to the climate of the country, the planting and harvest, etc.

Through concessions of this sort the liturgy itself goes through a period of adaptation and change. There is, moreover, another kind of legitimate and profitable experimentation possible, without permission from the Holy See. This is in the public exercises of piety which are not strictly liturgical.[47]

Thus, the many attempts to develop communal prayer and song at low Mass are expressly encouraged by the Congregation of Rites. These include the vernacular hymns which, provided they are sound in themselves and also suited to the individual parts of holy Mass, help to stir up community awareness in a way not possible through the objectively more excellent direct

[45] This indult was referred to in the September 3, 1958, Instruction of S.R.C. (cf. *supra*, note 8). The Instruction stated that particular exceptions to the liturgical use of Latin, conceded by the Holy See, retain their force (§ 12, c); that when celebrant, deacon, subdeacon or lector are allowed, in accordance with particular indults, to add the vernacular reading after the chant, the vernacular is to be read in a high and clear voice without authentic or improvised plain chant (§ 16, c); and that a "commentator" at a sung Mass may not substitute for the appointed ministers in this ritual reading after the chanted scriptural text (§ 96, e).

[46] While some places have long had the right to the use of Prefaces not in the Roman Missal, the reference is to new indults conceded by the Holy See.

[47] The 1958 Instruction (cf. *supra*, note 8) carefully distinguishes the *actiones liturgicae* found in the liturgical books approved by the Holy See from other exercises of piety, public or private, governed by the bishops (§§ 1; 12; cf. canons 1257 and 1259). Moreover, it clearly contemplates that at a less solemn liturgical service, specifically low Mass, that communal prayers and hymns be said or sung by the congregation, even though not found in the liturgical books and even though in the vernacular languages (§§ 14, b; 30). Such practices, again, are governed by the local ordinaries, although more difficult problems are to be submitted to the Holy See for solution (§§ 52, 53; cf. canon 1259, § 1).

liturgical participation, for which the Latin words of the Roman Missal must be used by the faithful.[48]

Here belong also the admirable combinations — for low Mass — of the English hymns with the Latin dialogue. The faithful recite the ordinary parts of Mass in unison with the celebrating priest, as well as make the brief responses; this is the "direct liturgical participation." Combined with this are three or four hymns in English suited to the Mass structure — at the beginning of Mass, during the Offertory of bread and wine, for the Communion procession, for the end of Mass.[49] These correspond roughly to the Introit, Offertory and Communion chants of sung Mass, and even to the Gradual and other verses between the Scripture Lessons. Because they are not "liturgical" in the strict sense, great flexibility is allowed to the pastor, rector, or celebrant.

This is true to an even greater extent in the case of devotional rites separated from the sacred liturgy itself but, it is hoped, always in harmony with it. These exercises of piety, such as evening devotions, allow for wide pastoral experimentation, always of course under the control of the bishops who may regulate all such rites not found in the liturgical books approved by the Holy See.[50]

Perhaps it may seem that such practices and devotions will only remotely influence liturgical development, but it is the accumulation of many influences and many petitions and indeed many discussions such as the present book which help the Roman pontiff to shape the sacred liturgy. Great as is the danger of unauthorized tampering with the liturgy, it seems even more

[48] The same Instruction lays down these principles very clearly (§ 14; 30–31). In §§ 14, b and 31 the direct liturgical participation through the use of the texts of the Roman Missal by the faithful — in response to, or in unison with, the celebrating priest — is considered. The addition of other prayers and songs is mentioned in § 14, b also and such prayers and songs — not "direct liturgical participation" — are referred to independently in § 30.

The insistence that all such *ad libitum* kinds of nondirect participation must be in harmony with the individual parts of Mass is found in § 30.

[49] Cf. preceding note.

[50] Canon 1259. The Holy See has taken (favorable) notice of attempts to include elements of a biblical and liturgical background in devotional exercises, subject to episcopal approval of new devotions. Cf. Bouscaren-O'Connor, *The Canon Law Digest*, 1958 Supplement (Milwaukee: Bruce, 1959), under canon 2. The question concerned so-called "biblico-liturgical vigils."

dangerous to neglect or to remain indifferent to the liturgical revival, restoration, and reform now happily in progress.

These many aspects of liturgical renewal are only part of the modern liturgical apostolate. On a wider basis and as a popular program, it is chiefly concerned with teaching the faithful the meaning of the sacred liturgy as it exists today, defective as it may appear to the experts and to the Holy See. That the faithful may here and now take part in the Mass and the sacraments with greater faith and devotion, with inner religious piety expressed through deed and song and prayer — these are the immediate purposes of the sacramental movement. At the same time, it is essential to have an eye to the future and contribute in however humble a fashion to the shape of the liturgy.

What has been said may be summed up: The liturgy offered to God by Jesus Christ and His members is, in its human elements, subject to change or modification. In the strictest sense, this is reserved to the Apostolic See, the see of Peter. Yet in the reform of sacred rites, the Holy See is and indeed must be aware of many influences and many contributions.

The chief of these influences will stem from the counsel and the requests of the bishops ruling their own dioceses and conscious of the needs of their flocks. Through the indults they receive from Rome a gradual development of the liturgy takes place before our eyes. And, in all the areas of worship not exactly regulated by the Holy See, the bishops have wide authority to encourage legitimate experimentation, for example, in the devotional practices which may one day find a place in the sacred liturgy.

All others charged with the cure of souls have a part in this development where practice and experience alone will demonstrate the needs of the worshiping community. But no one should forget the part already taken and still to be taken by the research, the study, the patient discussion of scholars. The present book is an example, the first thorough instance in the English language, of what this study is. It is addressed to both a general and a clerical audience; it is vital that clergy and faithful understand why changes come to pass and why Pius XII said that liturgical development is a testimony to the vigorous life of the Church.[51]

A final note is needed. It is easy to confuse stability and immutability, to canonize uniformity in place of unity. There is a desirable measure of uniformity, especially within a given rite of the Church, such as the Roman rite. But this principle must be applied in moderation; diversity too can be a proof of beauty and excellence, even when it is not almost a necessity.[52] Thus the Holy See requires a measure of uniformity within the Roman rite on the basis of the modern authentic liturgical books, but is satisfied with a substantial uniformity in other areas of worship, and vehemently opposes any uniformity which would be destructive of the non-Roman rites.

Stability, too, has obvious advantages in liturgical matters; it is inconceivable that the Church should return to improvised texts for the holy Canon, which would be thus made subject to frequent change. Yet the extreme or excess in the direction of stability is perhaps a graver peril, since it may lead to a static and formalized prayer almost totally unrelated to the spiritual sentiments of the worshiping Church. Therefore, we may reasonably expect that the ecclesiastical authority will pursue the course set by the late Pius XII and continue the gradual and fruitful progress of the liturgy.

After a long period of comparative inactivity in liturgical growth — made necessary by historical circumstances beyond the purposes of our discussion — the Holy See is at present engaged in a thorough reworking of sacred rites. When this is achieved after a period of years, the liturgy will still stand in need of growth and change. The very principles invoked above require this: while much of the liturgy is unchangeable because divine in origin, while much of the liturgy reflects legitimate and objectively sound developments of the past, there will always remain the hope that the living Church will find new prayers and rites the better to express her worship of almighty God.

FREDERICK R. MCMANUS

[51] *Mediator Dei* [§ 50], *loc. cit.*, pp. 541–542.
[52] Cf. John XXIII, encyclical letter, *Ad Petri cathedram* (June 29, 1959), AAS, 51 (1959), 514.

I Orientation

Purposes of This Book

THERE is more history hidden in this book than meets the eye of the reader. I originally planned an impersonal spectator's report on the scholarly discussions concerning the coming reconstruction of the Mass, backed by the appropriate apparatus of footnotes and references. But a prolonged illness delayed the project so long that there was ample time to let these plans simmer and mature. It was thus they came to their present shape. Instead of producing a monograph on the status of the discussion, I decided to write something more lively and personal, founded on the solid scholarship provided by the specialists in this field, but written rather from the pastoral point of view — an essay based on practical experience in many fields of priestly work, as well as forty years of active participation in the liturgical revival in two continents. Even though this book was actually written in 1957, it was not until June of 1959 that the revisions were completed.

As for myself, I first became involved in liturgical studies in 1919, as the result of reading Romano Guardini's *Spirit of the Liturgy*,[1] which has since become a classic. How I became more and more a part of the liturgical movement is a long story which I intend to tell in another book. For my purpose here it is sufficient to state that I have never lost contact with the literature in

[1] First published by Herder, (Freiburg, 1918). Available in English in Image Book ed. (Doubleday).

this field and have kept an eye on anything new and enlighten-
ing in this important territory. At no time has this been a hobby
or passing fad in my life, nor was I ever attracted by the mere
aesthetics of the thing. My concern with it has always been
essentially a pastoral one. It was the realization of the profoundly pastoral implications of the liturgical movement that
made it seem worth while to belong to a minority for almost
forty years. It was the vision of the Church, in her most intimate
self-understanding as the Body of Christ, become a lived and
experienced reality to her members, that impelled my colleagues
and myself to find new ways to open the closed world which
the liturgy had become — and in many ways still is — to the
Christian people, not archaic dilettantism, sheer joy of novelty,
or esoteric fadism.

It is reported that the late Pius XII, to whom we owe so much
in this field, told a group of European liturgists, about the year
1952, before one of their study meetings, that the liturgists had
tried with commendable success to bring the "people to the
Mass" by several devices like the dialog Mass in its various
forms, but that they had reached an impasse. It was now time,
he said, to "bring the Mass to the people by reform and adaptation," and before his time came to die he hoped to achieve so
much in this field that the advance would have become irrevers-
ible and would have laid down clear principles for future work.[2]
The differences between the renewed Holy Week Ordo (*Ordo
hebdomadae sanctae instauratus*, AAS, November 1955, cited
throughout as "OHSI") and the preceding 1570 version show
the principles guiding the work of restoration; and these principles are spelled out in the decrees, instructions, and articles
from the pens of responsible collaborators which accompanied the appearance of the OHSI. We can almost see the
dealings of Providence in the fact that Pius XII was granted the

    [2] See the general reforms advocated by Dom Thierry Maertens, O.S.B., in
his comprehensive article, "La célébration de la messe à la luminère des
directories récents," *Paroisse et Liturgie*, 39 (1957), 159 ff. (hereinafter:
"P&L"). A good general article on the reform of the Mass by the late
professor of moral theology at Munich University, Joseph Goettler, can also
be found in *Liturgisches Jahrbuch*, 7 (Münster, 1957), 39–64; especially,
45–47 and 59–60. The title of the article is: "Pia Desideria Liturgica."

opportunity to make a great part of the advance a matter of law when, on the feast of St. Pius X, September 3, 1958, a few weeks before he died, he commanded the publication of the famous "Instruction on Sacred Music and the Sacred Liturgy" (referred to hereafter as "Instruction"). What he said in 1952 that he hoped to carry out, was, therefore, at least partly accomplished before his death.

By now it ought to be common knowledge that a thorough reform of the Latin rite of the Catholic Church is being prepared — has, indeed, been under discussion since the time of St. Pius X. These discussions have already borne their first fruit. These are the reforms of the calendar,[3] the reforms contained in *Christus Dominus*,[4] and — most significant — the aforementioned restoration of Holy Week,[5] foreshadowed in 1951 by the facultative use of the Easter Vigil.

Like all the reforms contemplated by the supreme authority of the Church, these, which have already been carried out, were the result of long, open and frank discussion by scholars and pastors. Each incorporated two elements: pastoral needs and historical scholarship.

Proposals for reforms which are based on purely historical grounds, attempting to reconstruct the Mass in its "original" or "classical" form, must end up with some re-establishment of a synagogal prayer-service and of a primitive meal form of the Eucharist; unless, of course, an arbitrary limit is set to this process of going back to origins — the time of Gregory, say, or of Charlemagne. An equally unsatisfactory reform would result from exclusively pastoral considerations not nourished and guided by tradition; we would go aground in the same shallow waters of individualism in which so many other pious undertakings have been stranded.[6] The two elements, clearly, must find a balance, a tension, in any satisfactory solution.

[3] *Decretum generale* on reducing the rubrics to a simpler form, AAS, 47 (1955), 402–07; or the bull, *Abhinc duos annos*, AAS, 5 (1913), 449–51.
[4] Apostolic constitution, *Christus Dominus*, AAS, 45 (1953), 15.
[5] *Decretum generale, Maxima redemptionis*, AAS, 47 (1955), 838–47.
[6] Another possibility would be to leave the matter to experts in dogma and morals, but since such scholars have no special competence in the fields of liturgical reform or pastoral practice, the result would almost certainly

This discussion about reform, which is now more than two generations old, has also concerned itself with the Mass. This book, then, is an attempt to inform English-speaking Catholics about the state of the discussion and the kind of reforms which are most likely to result. Needless to say, while advocating such and such specific reforms is proper to liturgical conferences and journals, the actual decisions in this matter rest with the supreme authority of the Church.

I have made it a policy to incorporate the most advanced and logical proposals which have been made as the result both of research and pastoral needs, and I have done so because it seemed pointless to deal with any other than the most complete and profound of the various proposals.

By noting the most advanced of proposals for reform, I may well cause surprise in many readers. A tendency exists among priests and people alike to set great store on preserving the liturgy unchanged, simply for stability's sake. But the drastic reforms which the Holy See has already made indicate plainly that there is a sense of urgency in high places. It would be a mistake for us not to recognize that more reforms in the liturgy are impending.

And we should realize that this popular inclination to preserve the past unchanged has already had various unfortunate results. Some of the reforms which have been made recently seemed quite unexpected to many people; it became evident that an unprepared public may, in its temporary confusion, find it rather hard to collaborate enthusiastically with the intentions of the See of Peter.

For the sake of the future, therefore, it would be better if Catholics generally were given the means to understand the direction of liturgical thought, and thus were prepared for the changes which most surely are to come.

Ste Odile, Maria Laach, Louvain, Lugano, and Assisi are

---

resemble the work of Bernard Durst, O.S.B., for instance, which changes and transposes texts at will without regard either to tradition or to the theology of the Fathers. (*Das Wesen der Eucharistie*, Rome, 1953; reviewed adversely in ALW, 20, 1958.)

names which, in their liturgical significance, mean little to the average Catholic. But to hundreds of millions of Catholics in mission countries and behind the Iron Curtain, they will mean a great deal. For the liturgico-pastoral congresses, held in these places in recent years, have taken into consideration the many grave problems of Christian instruction and Christian worship which beset these peoples, and have proposed solutions for the consideration of the proper authorities.

The time has come for us also to concern ourselves with these same problems which are of the utmost urgency to our brother Catholics — problems which one day may be our own. The issues were grave enough to move Pius XII to launch a comprehensive program of reform, and they are becoming still graver as time goes on. Because of the loyalty and discipline we owe the Holy See, therefore, we need to become informed on this matter of impending changes; we must ourselves begin to realize the needs of our time, which are to be met by these reforms.[7]

What appears in this book is based on the thinking and findings of scholars on both sides of the Atlantic. Naturally the European material predominates in a field like this: after all, there are in Europe some two hundred million Catholics with innumerable ancient institutions of learning, while in the United States, we have only some forty to forty-five million Catholics and an academic tradition as yet young. Any kind of ecclesiastical isolationism or xenophobia is totally inadmissible in a field like this. The welfare of Latin-rite Christians on both sides of the Iron Curtain is at stake here, and we who live in freedom of worship, far from danger, must remember that we are a privileged minority. We can hardly begin to comprehend the problems besetting those who are hard pressed to preserve the faith, who need every means that can be offered them in their struggle to keep the faith alive — and not only alive, but ready to conquer. If nothing else could persuade us to take an interest in these questions and to consider them from a truly Catholic point

[7] See Appendix A for a summary of the conclusions of these congresses.

of view — we who have so many aids to full religious life — it should be the realization that Christians under atheistic pressure (either state-supported or more subtle) deeply need a kind of worship which will carry them to greater faith, to deeper participation in the Church's sacramental life, and to an undiluted reception of the Word. Such Christians are allowed no schools, almost no publications or organizations; they may meet, practically speaking, for worship only. Christian worship — above all, the Mass — of its nature can give them what they need so desperately. The proposed reforms are, then, for the purpose of enabling the intrinsic energies of the Mass to actually reach, inform, inspire, strengthen and transform the worshiping Christian of today.

We need not point to other countries exclusively to see why we should have a deep interest in a thorough reconstruction of our Mass. Among our own people, there is a need to put to better use the greatest source of evangelization and grace. I feel very uneasy when I see the superficial triumphs of enormously increased Communion figures without more indications of a concurrently deepening awareness of the setting of Communion in the Holy Sacrifice, of its implications as to our life in the Mystical Body, of its consequent social implications and so on. For is it not hard to say which is the more deadly: the harsh and visible control by the forces of totalitarianism, or the creeping and subtle erosion of our Christian substance by "conformity to the world" and the spiritual starvation of the people.

In the United States, enormous numbers of fine Catholics attend our Masses; the quantity of Communions is soaring. But are these *quantities* really reflected in our daily lives or in the social, economic, and cultural impact of Catholicism in our days? Is it not time for us to concern ourselves with the *quality* of Catholic life, with heroic spiritual lives, with profound and penetrating Catholicism? Our Lord gave us the means, the most noble means, before He died. He said, "Do this as my memorial." For all too many, the memorial-mystery is simply *mysterious*; all too many Catholics are mere onlookers at that which should be the greatest of their *acts*. To change these *spectators* into *participants* in the Banquet of the Church which contains the one and only Sacrifice is the ultimate aim of the proposed reforms.

Some readers may well ask whether participation has not been achieved by the Instruction of September, 1958. What is there to add, they may wonder. But this Instruction is in no way even a foreshadowing of the coming reconstruction of the Mass. It utilizes existing possibilities — those inherent in the Mass as we know it and in the existing laws and rubrics. The situation is, therefore, the same today as it was in 1952: the Instruction is concerned with bringing "the people to the Mass," not with "adapting the Mass for the use of the people"; its primary function was to create order out of chaos and to reestablish a basis for uniformity under the *existing* law. Naturally, it may have as a by-product the effect of laying the social and psychological foundation for the next step of "bringing the Mass to the people" but it is *not* the next step itself.

To prepare readers for this next step is my aim. That is the reason why I shall say nothing about better participation and better methods of doing what can now be done: my song is music of the future and my chief concern is to make people realize that my singing is part of a growing choir, not a solo. And not only that. I have a score to sing from; I am not improvising freely according to capricious fantasy.

I have no private wire to the authorities, neither am I disclosing any secret information. Occasionally I will venture forth on my own, and in all such cases, I will give ample warning beforehand. Otherwise all the proposed changes mentioned here have already been printed in books, magazines and conference proceedings. The scholarly work behind these proposals has been going on for many decades and is still going on today: it is useless to try to duplicate or improve the work of the experts. My task here is to make use of their results and to synthesize them for my readers.

Obviously, some of the proposed changes which I am including here may actually be incorporated into the "reformed" Mass when this is finally presented to Catholics of the Roman rite as another step in the great reform which started with St. Pius X and gathered new momentum under Pius XII. If this proves to be true, the reconstruction of the Mass which I am presenting will have served to give some idea of the actual Mass to come.

But even if all these suggestions are — as is also possible — bypassed or ignored, and my reconstruction thus proves to bear little resemblance to the reformed Mass rite of the future, it will nevertheless, I trust, have served the immediately useful purpose of enabling my readers to see the true essence of the liturgy of the Mass in clearer outlines — something which is not easily perceived in our present 1570 rite. In this connection, the French hierarchy noted in their *Directoire* (a foreshadowing of the Instruction) that it is desirable to distinguish between what is primary and secondary in the liturgy. For example, the psalm said at the foot of the altar should not be made to seem of equal importance with the Unde et memores or the Communicantes. (To clarify the confusion existing in our present rite was not the business of the Instruction and the problem was ignored in its setting out of the different stages of the dialog Mass.) One of the chief purposes of all proposed reforms, then, is to restore and bring out clearly the essential structure and line of action of the Mass. And this is also one of my chief purposes in this book.

The Latin and English "text" of a sample Mass as reconstructed along the lines I am going to describe is given in Chapter Five to aid the reader's imagination and to give flesh and bones to what would otherwise be a series of abstract proposals. This text is, obviously, meant only to serve as a basis for thought, study and discussion. As I said above, I have no advance information as to what measures will actually be adopted in the end. But *discussion* of reform measures has been going on for decades; the fact that the average Catholic has not been, and is not aware of the discussion was not the result of any desire to keep the subject a secret, but simply of the fact that much of the material has not been easily available outside a circle of experts.

When I mention "discussion," together with study and thought, I do not mean that, as a result of reading this book, fruitful new suggestions will be made by groups of persons who cheerfully admit their lack of expert knowledge. Nor do I look forward to an avalanche of petitions which, because of the complexity of most of the issues, would result only in confusion. The question here is not one of lobbying or of the "preparation of legislation by democratic process"; it is one of becoming informed about an important stage of liturgical development and of stimulating further study. If the available books by Jungmann, Ellard, Parsch, O'Shea and Murphy, together with the magazine *Worship,* are studied by more people and with a greater feeling of relevancy, I shall feel that my book has accomplished a great deal.

I do, however, hope for another result as well. And this is a keener awareness of tradition and historical growth and, in consequence, the cultivation of a more receptive attitude toward needed reforms and adjustments. If some of the latest reforms caused bewilderment among loyal Catholics, it was in great part due to lack of sufficient preparation of their minds. I hope, therefore, that this book, by spelling out in specific detail what may possibly happen, will stimulate the reader's imagination and prevent him from thinking when the reform actually does come, "Why didn't someone tell me what was going on?"

What the uninitiated reader may find startling at first in the proposals embodied in this book will not seem so surprising in the end: he will find that they all hang together. And he will realize that it is better that he be astonished now by something which seems novel but which he will find to be well reasoned, than it would be to remain uninformed and so to allow the finished reform to shock him when it comes, which will be precisely when his full cooperation will be called for and needed.

And there is another point: there is still time to discuss the reforms, to bring details to the attention of the bishops and thus to Rome. It is crucial, therefore, to start the study, to begin quiet and mannerly discussion now, in order to prevent the reproach later on that we are being served with the results of European needs and promptings only. If this were to happen, if the idea were to spread that we were not consulted, there would almost certainly be a scramble for dispensations, exceptions and delays; or, worse, resistance and coolness toward measures which were designed to kindle enthusiasm, relief, and a new vigor in the sacramental life that would bear apostolic fruit.

Background

What we now use as our Roman Missal was published by the Holy See at the request of the Council of Trent. Its publication, ordered by, and given out under the name of, St. Pius V after the council had adjourned, took place in 1570. This Missal was made mandatory for the Latin Rite, with few exceptions, and thus "froze" the hitherto fluid Missal. Up to the revision of the Holy Week rites in 1956, only minor changes, almost all in the calendar, had been made in the nearly four hundred years since the original publication.

Up until 1570, the Latin Mass rite was not subject to the strict regulation we are accustomed to today. Each church used its own Mass-books compiled from traditional sources. Thus many slight variations existed on the general pattern of the "Roman" rite, which was itself, like the other major rites of the Church all over the world, a result of many centuries' growth and development from the original pattern of the Last Supper and the Jewish synagogue service. No positive law existed to prevent arbitrary changes. It was to prevent such changes and developments, which by the fifteenth century were becoming wild and unregulated, that the Council of Trent called for the publication of one Missal to be imposed on all the churches of the Latin rite, with some few exceptions. This "freezing" was undoubtedly providential, since at that time there was little understanding of the spirit of the liturgy or of its laws and history, and any changes that might have been made could hardly have been for the better.

The Missal of 1570, for the most part, reproduced the Missal of the papal *ceremoniarius,* Burkhard, which had appeared and gathered support a hundred years earlier, being, in turn, a reorganized and systematized collection of earlier versions. On the whole, it was a hurried composition and a compromise; it was never intended to be a creative liturgical work. Moreover, it took little account of either historical or pastoral considerations — though this was, perhaps, inevitable in the state of historical knowledge of the liturgy and the general circumstances of the time.

If one could measure the impact of forces outside the liturgy itself which contributed to shaping the Roman Mass from its sub-apostolic beginnings up to the fifteenth century — and do the same for all the other liturgies — the development of dogma would loom large. But such also seemingly less important factors as the introduction of unleavened bread, the exclusion of vernacular languages, the clerical character of the monastic centuries and the suppression, unnoticeable and gradual as it was, of the chalice for the Communion of the laity, would loom larger than current apologetics usually makes them seem. For example, who would have "exposed" and enthroned the species of a host made of *leavened* bread? No wonder this was not done earlier or in the Eastern rites! Another factor was the scholastic thinking of the High Middle Ages: its speculations removed all inhibitions about, and even justified, the suppression of the chalice for the laity, which had earlier been regarded merely as a practical measure of convenience. And what a large role must we ascribe to the devout popularizing of the mystics, from Bernard to Ruysbroeck, and their counterpart in the *Devotio moderna*? For instance, when the "Presence" experienced by the mystics in solitude and in the Dark Night of the senses gradually became "located" in the Blessed Sacrament, and the colloquy between the naked soul and the Living God became, in popular preaching, a "visit" and colloquy with Jesus present in the sanctuary of any church, then the atmosphere had been created for the low Mass and the silent congregation, and also for the devout to regard sacramental Communion as the exception and as an intensified mystical experience. Jansenism gave all this a sinister and forbidding background, but the rare Communion of the devout — not to speak of the lax and the indifferent and the sinful — is much older than the *Augustinus* of Bishop Jansenius.

Compare the early liturgy of Hippolytus of Rome or Justin Martyr or St. Augustine with that of the 1570 Missal, and it is obvious that each corresponds to the cultural conditions and spiritual attitudes of its own way. It also becomes clear that the forms of the fifteenth century are now in need of new adaptation.

The desire for liturgical reform goes back to the days of such seventeenth-century liturgical scholarship as that of the Benedictines of St. Maur. Louis Bouyer in his now near-classic *Liturgical Piety* (Notre Dame, Indiana, 1955), has a good résumé of these vigorous early movements. The second half of the ninteenth century and the early twentieth century are also lucidly summarized in this same book. Duchesne, Doelger, Quasten, Casel, Mohlberg, Battifol, Capelle, Botte, Heiming, Chavasse, Jungmann, Bugnini, O'Shea, Michel, Kennedy, Hanssens, are names picked at random from a host of modern scholars. While most of them have labored mainly to sift the wheat from the chaff and to throw a light on the history of the liturgy, some of them have also proposed adaptations, the weeding out of superfluous and obscuring growth, and measures to meet the needs of modern parishioners and to make sacramental participation possible.

It would be odious to pick heroes from this tradition, but none among them have had the influence of Dom Lambert Beauduin and Joseph A. Jungmann. Many of the latest reforms go back to the work of these two men. Scholars and pastors met and discussed their proposals, first in small groups and at quiet meetings at Ste Odile, France; at Maria Laach, Germany; at Louvain, Belgium; then in larger groups and with more publicity, at Lugano, Switzerland, and finally in a World Congress at Assisi and Rome in 1956. A remarkable aspect of these efforts by individuals and groups is that in one way or another

full discussion was encouraged by the Holy See. Not only were representatives of the Sacred Congregation of Rites present, but so were cardinals of the curia and of prominent sees, and there was always a letter of approval sent from the highest authorities. It is therefore past time for us to be informed of what should be by now common knowledge.

Let there be no misunderstanding: these liturgical gatherings and writings are not *agents* of reform. By positive law, since Trent, only the Holy See can execute suggestions submitted by the proper authorities — i.e. the hierarchy, can sift, select, and reject or accept whatever has been proposed.[8] Rome listens carefully, but selects and acts in her own wisdom. There are no lobbyists or "pressure groups" involved. The votes that are taken among the members of the hierarchy throughout the world are secret: the hierarchy are the real advisers, while scholars and conferences might be called the "suggestors."

There is no similarity between this process and the procedures of modern democratic life, although no one can deny that the "demos — people" have silently or articulately spoken through action, abstention, and acclaim. The Church's method of assessing the needs and desires of the common man differs

[8] How grave a matter unauthorized "anticipated" reform — that is, actually carrying out the Mass or any other liturgical rite in any way other than that prescribed in the official liturgical texts — can become is clear from the recent *Commonitio* (*De non introducendis novis ritibus in divina officia*, AAS, 50 [1958], 114). The commentary on this document by the noted liturgical expert A. Bugnini, C. M., in *Ephemerides Liturgicae*, 57, II, pp. 137 ff., makes clear what the Sacred Congregation of the Holy Office had in mind in its strictures: Diaconal litanies at the Offertory; addition of a third lesson from the Old Testament; an unusual and over-solemn rite of bringing the Gospel-book to the altar; standing instead of kneeling at the Elevation; simultaneous elevation of the sacred species of bread and wine; pronunciation of the final Amen at the "Little Elevation" instead of after it; new forms of hosts; omission of the Confiteor before the people's communion or of the prayers at the foot of the altar except where these were actually abolished in the OHSI; omission of the last Gospel at all Masses; omission of the words "*Mysterium Fidei*" from the words of institution. As these examples of innovations and unauthorized restitutions — although according to the spirit of the latest reforms — show, extraordinary things have been going on in Europe, reminding one of the reforms of Abbé Jubé in the seventeenth century and dangerously close to what happened at Pistoia. This *Commonitio* does not pass on the intrinsic *worth* of the changes — what is condemned is in any way anticipating the action of the proper authorities in this regard. We are quite free to wish and to pray that at least the best of them may be authorized, as has already been foreshadowed in the OHSI of 1955.

from that of the state; yet the reforms are not made in a vacuum, but as the result of suggestions made as above and with a finger on the pulse of the people. The friends of archaic forms, the *"laudatores temporis acti,"* in short those who dream of a past golden age of a perfect liturgy are not the instigators: history is consulted to insure continuity of form, to guarantee that the wisdom of the past guides and inspires, and to prevent arbitrariness.

Guiding Rules of This Presentation

1. The likelihood of a reform is assumed: it is evident from a long series of documents and actions (e.g., OHSI, *Christus Dominus*, etc.).

2. The principal basis for this presentation are the international conferences of liturgical scholars held in Ste Odile, Maria Laach, Louvain, Lugano, etc., and the available literature (Jungmann, Chavasse, Botte, Bouyer, etc.,).

3. Preserve intact what tradition has wrought, unless weighty considerations advise change.

4. There is a tendency to *cumulation*, to heap prayer on prayer, as in the present Offertory, and in the blessings of ashes, palms, fire, etc., and so to obscure the essential outlines of the Mass until they have become unrecognizable; these excrescences should be eliminated.

5. The clearer the essential outline of the Mass becomes, the better.

6. Since parish liturgy is for the parishioners, it should be made as lucid and simple as possible without oversimplifying its nature as a mystery — the word used in its liturgical sense, as we find it in the Missal (This does not mean "mysteriousness": see Appendix D) — or losing its dignity, and its beauty.

7. Empty and now meaningless rites, excessive allegorism, wordiness, and foreign elements should be eliminated.

8. The structural lines and the main points of emphasis should be unmistakable; an instructed and believing Christian should no longer be confused, for instance, by such details as

the almost inexplicable rite with the empty paten after the Pater noster or by similar archaic remnants.

9. A maximum of participation should be made possible, with a proper division of functions: the laity are no longer silent spectators, nor do they take over the role of any of the sacred ministers. The amorphous crowd should become again an ordered congregation with a rightful function. (This is strongly supported by the Instruction of September, 1958, but the maximum possibilities are not attained in this temporary arrangement).

10. What was originally derived from the synagogal service — entrance rite, instruction, common prayer, meditation — should be distinguishable from the Sacrifice-Banquet: it should be held *in choro*, not at the altar itself.

11. There appears to be a general desire to re-establish the spirit of the Last Supper and the synaxes as described in Holy Writ (Acts) and the Fathers: this means freeing the core of sacramental worship from all unnecessary pomp. (This applies only to parish worship. Monasteries, cathedrals, and other centers of great and magnificent celebrations are not affected.)

12. There is a serious danger of overshooting the aim, once one embarks on the exhilarating task of putting things in order. Room must be left for "solemnity," to avoid triteness, a romantically conceived "evangelical simplicity," formless individualism, or the victimizing of the congregation by a tasteless and uninspired mystagogue. All that is noble and dignified, all that rises above ephemeral inspiration, must be preserved. The Roman liturgy is *magnanimous*, solemn, sober, and warm: it should never lose these qualities, even when carried out in the smallest chapel.

13. The text of the sample Mass is based on the recommendations of the various liturgical conferences (see Appendix A), and is in strict conformity in spirit and in externals with the details of the last Roman reforms: the restored Holy Week (OHSI); the interim calendar and the Instruction. My readers

will therefore find the following changes in accordance with the reforms of Pius XII:

a) *Oremus* before any prayer (Collect, Postcommunion) will indicate a short but noticeable space of time for silent, individual prayer by the clergy and the people (OHSI).

b) Responses will be made communally: "All respond" wherever the liturgy requires this. No longer will the responding be done within the clerical circle around the altar only, nor will it be delegated to "deputies of the people" like servers and choirs (Instruction, 1958).

c) Processionals like the "entrance" of the priest (formerly the Introit), Offertory and Communion will be identified as such: they will be called "Antiphon for . . ." followed by a psalm or verses as the case may be (Instruction, 1958).

d) Division of functions and roles will be made visible, especially in avoiding a duplicate or triplicate reading of the same text by different ministers, e.g., when the deacon chants the Gospel, all, including the celebrant, listen (*auscultant*) (OHSI).

e) The choir will accordingly lead the congregation; it will not substitute for the congregation's rightful part, and it will render as its own special contribution only those parts which were not meant for congregational singing (like the Gradual and the more difficult Offertory Antiphons) (OHSI).

f) Typography: larger type in Roman letters will be used for the audible and essential parts of the Mass, while small print will be used for those parts which are of strictly sacerdotal devotion, or which may possibly be made *ad libitum* and no longer obligatory, or which merely accompany the actions of the ministers (Munda cor, Per evangelica dicta, Offertory prayers, etc.).

New Classification of Masses

Since the publication of the Instruction, an authoritative way exists of classifying the different types of Mass. The future reform is, of course, not bound by a document which intends to regulate an existing condition without reforming it, but I think that we can safely assume that, outside of minor details, this classification will remain even after the reform. It is a division suggested by new developments, that of dialog Mass, for instance, and it became necessary to dam the rising flood of formulas for this new development. The difficulty for me, is to find a term for the rightfully banished "private" Mass. What it really is, is a public Mass, as all Masses are public in essence, performed for devotion's sake under circumstances of privacy, that is, in a chapel or at an altar where only one representative of the public assists, either as an acolyte or a silent worshiper. (These Masses are common in parishes as well as in religious houses, and as long as concelebration is forbidden, we will have them, and we have to include them in our thinking.) "Minimally participated Masses" does not sound acceptable. "Private" in English does not sound as formidably "deprived" as *privata* does in Latin, but the Instruction is definite about forbidding or at least counseling against the use of the term "private Mass." Neither does "low Mass," "silent or read Mass" cover the case satisfactorily. I will therefore take refuge in the neutral term "devotional Mass."

Hitherto the Mass was either a low Mass (private or public, without solemnity) or a chanted Mass in one of its several different forms. The texts are identical. The celebrant reads the same texts whether it is a pontifical or a low Mass. There is a scant regard for the functional character of the parts of the Mass or of the roles of the ministers: high Mass is a sung low Mass, and low Mass a recited high Mass; the congregation listens to both with varying degrees of (private) devotion. The OHSI has fortunately made short shrift of this, and has re-established a sacred and logical order, though this pertains only to the Holy Week rites themselves.

There remain as before two types of sung Masses (*Missae in Cantu*): (1) Solemn Mass — Priest, deacon, subdeacon if available, servers, choir-schola, and participating congregation. (2) Chanted Mass — Priest, lector and other servers, choir-schola, and participating congregation.

There are also now two types of "low, read or spoken Masses"; of which the second type has two divisions: (1) Recited Mass — Priest, lector, commentator, servers, responding and fully externally participating congregation. (2) Low Mass without participation: (a) Priest, server and silent congregation. (b) Priest, server, and no visible congregation outside a minimal representation of one or a few. This is what we will call the "devotional Mass."

Although the Instruction leaves room for these two types of "read Mass," the emphasis is on the other types of Mass. I do not foresee that the "devotional Mass" will be abolished by a future reform and have therefore included it in my diagrams.

Proper Division of Roles

The celebrant at sung Mass will only sing or read those texts which were his in the original sacramentaries, those which are strictly sacerdotal and "presidential": the acclamations, the orations, the blessings, the consecratory parts (Canon and Communion), absolutions, etc. He will *not* read the texts which properly are those of the deacon, the ministers, the choir or the congregation. His role is thus elevated, focused upon purely sacerdotal functions.

As we descend from the most perfect form of worship, sung Mass, the priest gradually takes over the function of others: he reads the subdeacon's (lector's) Lesson, the deacon's Gospel, and in the absence of lectors, choir, and congregation (as in a "devotional Mass") he takes over also what normally would be their functions. The more perfect form of Mass is that with fully distinguished roles and division of functions.

The deacon at Mass chants the Gospel, dismisses the congregation; chants *Flectamus genua* and *Humiliate*; assists at the Offertory preparation of the gifts and gives Communion with the celebrant. In general, he helps the celebrant.

The subdeacon at Mass chants the Epistle or Lesson, assists at the preparation of the chalice and host (no longer *Patenarius*); bears the processional cross; is in charge of the lower

40   ORIENTATION

assistants in the sanctuary as distinct from the deacon's role of assisting the priest.

The Servers carry out the acolytes' service and at a "devotional" Mass substitute for a congregation. At a recited Mass, they may also act as lectors (Epistle, etc.). But so long as a congregation is present, they may not be the sole respondents. The congregation should not deputize the servers to perform the task of making the responses in its stead, a condition, although implicitly disapproved by OHSI and happily corrected by the 1958 Instruction, still all too common.

The choir, or schola, has received due attention in the Instruction. The following is, therefore, mainly a recapitulation of the rules given therein and hardly goes beyond them. Where the choir maintains its soloist position, it is understood that the congregation sings at least the short responsorial parts. The choir members should know that they are to *lead* the congregational singing, not to substitute for a silent congregation. They will, however, also sing those proper parts which are too elaborate for the congregation and which are meant to be listened to: the antiphons for the entrance, Offertory and Communion processionals, Gradual, etc. Such difficult compositions as the Gradual were always reserved to trained soloists. I do not think that the congregation should take over *all* there is to sing outside the sacred ministers' parts.

The choir's role in a well-developed parish may be to alternate with the congregation in singing the Ordinary of the Mass. This practice maintains a certain quality in the congregational singing, for otherwise deterioration is apt to set in from habit and because of the peculiarities developed by singing crowds. When the schola maintains rhythm and melody it serves as an implicit educational factor. This should, however, never lead to the schola's usurpation of the entire Ordinary of the parish's sung Mass. The choir has ample opportunity to show its ability in the Proper. The choir's location is not in a distant loft behind and above the congregation, but either in a "pit" (as in the old basilicas — Santa Sabina, Santa Maria in Cosmedin, or, best of all, San Clemente with its two ambos) or behind a louvered screen to the right or left of the altar (this is already done in many American churches).

Lay readers and leaders. Using the Instruction as a starting point and progressing from it in the same direction, the following seems to be indicated:

At sung Masses, wearing cassock and surplice or simple alb and cincture, they will sing the Epistle and then read its translation (Prophecies, Lessons). At recited parish Masses, they will read the Epistle, intone choral parts and lead the congregational recitation (Introit Antiphon, Psalm, and wherever else leadership or reading is needed or advisable). Several readers can form a *chorus* to respond to the congregation — e.g., at the entrance, a leader recites the Antiphon, the congregation repeats it, the leader recites the Psalm, alternating it with the congregation's repetition of the Antiphon until the clergy are ready for the Kyrie. The same could be done at the Offertory and Communion. These functions correspond to those of the ordained lector. This contributes to the training of laymen in the spirit of Catholic action and the lay apostolate. Its pastoral purpose is the better integration of the parish.

Adaptation of Church Interior and Sanctuary

Like all the other proposals, this sketch is tentative and based on the necessities developed in the body of the text. This is quite evident in the hesitation about the location of the bench for the ministers.

The adaptations discussed require very little alteration of churches, and such changes as they necessitate are based on historical precedent and a sound Roman tradition. The matter will have to be covered by new rubrics, which are anticipated to a minor degree in the recent OHSI (e.g., the relocation of the paschal candle and the celebrant's place during the Lessons). I remain general and rather vague, as this question is in the discussion stage, but a few minimum requirements can be surmised:

The parish church as a whole. There should be clear emphasis on congregational participation in parish churches, which means removal of obstructions and emphasis on essentials. The choir must be relocated (near the altar) to serve in its traditional capacity and to preclude the "concert" atmosphere of "performing" for the parish. The pulpit, where it exists, must be brought into the sanctuary or close to it. There must be a clear distinction between the nave and the sanctuary, to make physically visible the distinction of functions. No invasion of the sanctuary by the congregation, and no physical movement of the sacred ministers into the space allocated to the people should take place, except in processions, and so on.

The sanctuary. The altar should become the emphatic locus for the Banquet-Sacrifice; no longer should it be an enlarged lectern or a base for ornate furnishings. The number of candles upon it ought to be determined by the rite of the Mass. Unlighted (dead) candles should be removed. The "choral" part

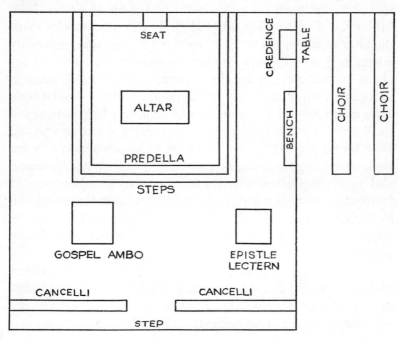

of the sanctuary would best serve a newly emphasized congregational participation in the parish if there were the following changes and additions:

An Epistle lectern not too far from the altar rails (*cancelli*).

A Gospel ambo (or pulpit) opposite the lectern (the ancient Roman basilicas had this provision — e.g., San Clemente), both facing the congregation.

The bench for the clergy so arranged that part of the rite can be performed at it. (See, e.g., OHSI on Good Friday).

A larger credence table, also visible to the congregation, which bears vestments (chasuble, tunics, etc.) during the Fore Mass, and is used to prepare the host and chalice at the Offertory, thus shutting out the notion that the Offertory is anything more than a preparing of the gifts), and to hold books, cruets, patens, bell, etc.

The altar facing the congregation. I am glad to say that my doubts about its historical and doctrinal feasibility have been solved by the compact and careful treatment of Father John Miller, C.S.C. (*Worship*, 33 [1959], 83 ff.). I personally favor the altar at which the priest faces the congregation, especially when, as is now the case, he acts as reader and leader of the chant or recitation. After the reform, if it is carried through according to the discussion here summarized, this consideration loses its urgency: the reading would no longer be performed at the altar, but at the lecterns near and facing the congregation. Now for all practical purposes the reading celebrant faces the wall, addressing himself to no audience. The doctrinal, pastoral, and psychological reasons for a return to the older way of facing the congregation even during the Banquet-Sacrifice given by Father Miller are so convincing that I hope that this will be made the normal position for the priest. However, there is one problem which is hard to solve: the location of the tabernacle.

According to the present rubrics, the location of the tabernacle, its size and its symbolism have been laid down in a recent decree of the Congregation of Rites. There is, therefore, not much to be said at the present stage, but I hope that the discussion is still open for a return to the older tradition after the reform. Even now, the celebrant ignores the tabernacle through the entire Mass. This can easily be verified by comparing the elaborate rules for turns and genuflections when Mass is said before the Blessed Sacrament exposed (and remember that this is only allowed in certain cases), with the rules at ordinary Masses. The Holy Eucharist is treated as absent during the liturgy, as eminently present for private devotion. Would it therefore be altogether novel if the logical step were taken of removing the tabernacle to a better place on a special "Altar of the Blessed Sacrament"? This is already the law for churches with liturgical choir office — cathedrals and abbey churches — and at any pontifical high Mass. Since modern piety has surrounded the reserved Blessed Sacrament with an aura of intimacy and personal warmth, a special chapel, or at least a special altar, would actually contribute to the trend and keep the two spheres neatly separated to the advantage of both. For practical reasons, the tabernacle in parish churches should be near the sanctuary: in case of Communions more numerous than expected, additional hosts must be available for distribution. We must remember that not only tradition, but two pontiffs, Benedict XIV and Pius XII, have reminded us that the faithful should receive Holy Communion from the supply consecrated at the Mass they participate in and not (normally) from a store of hosts consecrated beforehand (*Mediator Dei*).

Procedure

Now we are ready to get to the heart of our material. We shall first present the proposed changes in each part of the Mass by means of five schemata, followed by explanatory notes. In the second chapter we will treat of the Entrance Rite, i.e., from the (Asperges and) Entrance Procession to the Amen after the Collect, and the Service of the Word, i.e., from the (Old Testament Lesson through the) Epistle and Gospel to the Amen after the Bidding Prayers. In the third chapter we will cover the Offertory, i.e., from the Nicene Creed to the Amen after the

Super oblata (Secreta), and the Anaphora or Canon, i.e., from the Preface to the Amen after the Great Doxology. The fourth chapter will be devoted to the Communion Rite, i.e., from the Our Father to the Amen after the Last Blessing.

A sample Mass text, incorporating these changes, will constitute the fifth chapter. The text will be in English throughout, with the exception of the Canon which will furnish both the English and the Latin texts. The "rubrics" of this Mass are sketchy and general, limited to what is necessary to visualize the proposed changes. Where I am in doubt, an alternate solution will be given in the footnotes.

In a treatment such as this, one cannot treat of everything; I have restricted myself to the parochial Mass and its problems, omitting a discussion of forms for cathedrals and collegiate churches. Other questions are still more obviously beyond the scope of this book, although allied to it; hence the omission of such matters as calendar reform, the true meaning of the liturgical year, and so on.

II Contemplated Reforms in the Area
of the Present Fore Mass

The Entrance Rite

The Entrance Rite [1] — in our present Mass hardly separate from the Service of the Word — has a definite and distinct purpose in the whole of the Mass: It offers a solemn and inspiring introduction to the Mass celebration and makes coming into the Presence of God a living experience to the individual and the assembled parish family. Its pattern is obvious: A short halt at the baptistery to renew in a visible rite (the Asperges) the spirit of our own baptism. A stately procession by the clergy to the altar accompanied by singing, the solemn greeting of the altar, then a majestic Kyrie, the royal acclamation to the King whose Body we are, the Gloria joins with the angels in praising God, the whole concluded by the silent prayer of all, summed up by the celebrant's Collect and the people's Amen.

All of this is our response to the call from on high and a first taking shape of the *Ecclesia*, the "Called."

1. The Asperges.[2] This rite becomes more meaningful if it is not a duplicate of the entrance procession (as is now the

---

[1] Dom Maertens distinguishes the following parts of the Mass: *1*) Entrance Rite; *2*) Liturgy of the Word; *3*) Offertory; *4*) Canon; *5*) Communion. He reports in P&L (39 [1957], 164) that the use of the term, "Entrance Rite," was officially adopted by the Dioceses of Bologna, Namur and Tournai. (On Ember Wednesdays and Saturdays the Collect of the day precedes the first Lesson.)

[2] The Asperges at the font is discussed in Fr. Chery's description of the parochial Mass at St. Severin in Paris; there, the celebrant recites the Asperges or the Vidi without Psalm or Collect.

Everything takes place in the sanctuary (in choro) unless otherwise indicated.

	Solemn Mass	Chanted Mass	Recited Mass	Devotional Mass
Pre-Mass: Iudica and Confiteor	sacristy*	do.*	do.*	altar
1. Asperges (Vidi)	Performed by cel. & ministers near gate of baptistery*			
2. Antiphon and Psalm of Introit procession (en route*)	schola and* cong.	do.*	lector* and cong.	cel.
3. Kyrie at altar steps* and sedilla*	choir & cong. alternate*	do.*	cel. & cong. alternate*	cel. & server
4. Gloria (at the bench*); (less frequently than now*)	cel. intones; choir & cong. alternate	do.	cel. intones; lector* & cong. alternate	cel.
5. Dominus vobiscum (at the bench*) Et cum spiritu tuo Oremus (pause*) Collect (one only)	cel. cong.* cel. cel.	do. do.* do. do.	do. do.* do. do.	cel. (at the altar) server do. do.
6. Amen	all*	do.*	do.*	server

*Features that are either new, in a new setting or derived from principles ruling OHSI. "Ditto" is abbreviated "do." to conserve space.

_____SCHEMA I_____

case), but is integrated into it and relocated. The procession of the clergy leaves the sacristy, proceeds by a side aisle to the baptistery. Here the deacon takes the aspergile from the holy water container of the baptistery, and hands it to the celebrant who sprinkles the assistants and the congregation. The Introit Antiphon and Psalm, as described below, are sung throughout the procession of the clergy.

2. *The Entrance Procession.*[3] When the sprinkling is finished,

[3] The so-called "prayers at the foot of the altar" would be made optional as a private preparation of the celebrant, and recited in the sacristy. This is what they were originally and this is their character. They can take the place of the highly allegorical vesting prayers. If we take high Mass as the proto-

the clergy continue the procession to the altar. The manner of singing is as follows: The choir intones the Introit Antiphon. The congregation repeats a short refrain. Then the Psalm is sung by the choir or cantor; after every second verse, the congregation repeats the refrain.[4] As soon as the procession reaches the

type of all Masses, we notice that in the present unreformed Mass, the prayers at the foot of the altar "fight" with the singing of the Introit and make for distraction. The medieval tendency to accumulate prayers and "apologias" led to the insertion of these prayers at this place at a rather late date. Father J. A. Jungmann, S.J., in his program for the reconstruction of the Mass (Lugano, September 16, 1953), proposed that the Confiteor in some form, e.g., in the shorter form of the Dominican Rite, should be located after the Service of the Word and before the Anaphora. He gives some excellent reasons for this re-arrangement, some of them are pastoral, some liturgical.

According to him, the present double Confiteor (before Mass for the priest, before Communion for the communicants) is liturgically not too fortunate, as it violates one of the basic rules of good liturgy: not to repeat itself and not to place a formula mechanically, out of context. It is obvious that the second Confiteor was introduced from the Communion rite outside Mass, at a time when Communion was regarded as detached from the proceeding Mass; the priest does not repeat his Confiteor; only the laity and ministers do so, as if they had not participated in the foregoing parts of the Mass. (At ordination this is not the case: the concelebrating *ordinati* receive Holy Communion as the pontiff does.)

The present first Confiteor is of little value for the faithful, since those who need it most, i.e., the late comers and the unprepared, are either not present or not psychologically in the best disposition to perform an act of conscious contrition. According to Jungmann, then, the moment best suited for the confession of sinfulness is:

1) When the participants have been properly disposed for so weighty an action, which is normally after having listened to the ideal image of a Christian given them by the words of Scripture and the sermon, and after the prayers that had preceded these instructional parts, they can grasp the chasm between their redeemed state and their insufficiency better than ever at this moment.

2) Before the whole Anaphora, the Sacrifice-Banquet, in which they are to participate as the *Q'hal Yavé* or *Ecclesia Dei*, freed from sins and imperfections by the absolution and their act of contrition *in globo*. This makes for participation with the celebrant throughout the whole Anaphora, and not for admission to the "cleansed" only after the priest's Communion. Father Jungmann gives an impressive array of reasons; from a viewpoint of pastoral liturgy this seems another example of his acute sense of timing and of lifting the liturgical formula out of its "performance" stage into the realm of personalized prayer.

The most impressive reason, apart from the practico-pastoral ones, seems to be the visible removal of the present impression that the participation of the faithful is ignored up to the very moment of their admission to Holy Communion, as if they had been allowed to pray whatever they wanted to up to this stage of final admission to the mysteries. To remove this Confiteor — if Father Jungmann's suggestion is followed in this detail — would be a more convincing gesture than a thousand assertions that the laity "really have a part to play" in the Mass: action speaks louder than words.

[4] In case it is necessary to vary this procedure, the psalms or suitable hymns have been suggested for the procession. The latter would have to be selected

altar the celebrant ascends to and kisses the altar and then descends to the bench in the sanctuary.

In a dialog Mass, the singing would consist of appropriate hymns or psalms or the reciting of the Entrance Psalm, the congregation alternating with the reader or the celebrant. At solemn Mass, incense is carried during the procession. According to the class of the rite, two, four or six candles are carried in the procession, to be used as altar candles. The processional cross is carried by the subdeacon (acolyte in sung Mass and recited Mass) and also used as the altar cross. The salutation of the altar by the celebrant could be amplified at solemn Mass by the incensation (around the altar) before the celebrant descends to his place at the bench.

3. *The Kyrie eleison.* After arriving at the bench, the celebrant intones the Kyrie eleison, which is then alternated between the schola and congregation as follows:

1	2	3	4	5
cel.	cong.	schola	cong.	schola

6	7	8	9
cong.	schola	cong.	all

4. *The Gloria* is intoned by the celebrant; it is suggested that it be less frequently used: on Sundays and what are now doubles of the first and second class. The Gloria is also alternated by the schola and congregation: the sacred ministers stand at the bench and join in the singing.

5. *Collect*, preceded by the customary salutation and concluded by the Amen of the congregation. Between the Oremus and the body of the Collect, the pause now re-established by OHSI as a period for recollection and for private prayer should be made general.[5] The importance and weight of this prayer seems to require that no commemoration or *imperata* be added. The multiplication of unconnected formulas detracts from their individual impact. Where to have *imperata*? During the new

---

very carefully to fit the spirit of the rite, the day or feast, and the season of the year. The new rubrics would have to settle the alternate proposals.
[5] On the pause after the Oremus, see OHSI and P&L, 19 (1937), 175.

"Bidding" or Litany Prayers, modeled after the Good Friday intercessions.[6]

6. *The Amen* fitly concludes the opening unit of the Mass which, together with the Service of the Word, grew out of the synagogal service of the postexiliary Jewish liturgy and later was joined with the Holy Synaxis of the Mass.

Vestments worn during the Entrance Rite. At the Lugano Conference in September, 1953, it was my impression that a number of its members, including, if I remember correctly, Father Jungmann, proposed it as fitting that the sacred ministers should vest in chasuble, dalmatic and tunic *only* for the actual sacrificial part of the Mass — in other words after the Fore Mass is over — to show the different spirit of the two components of the Mass.

This needs further discussion. Unless all priests can be persuaded to use well-fitted linen albs, most of us would seem to be appearing in "undress." A way out would be for the celebrant to wear a cope until the end of the sermon and bidding prayers, while the deacon could wear a suitable deacon's stole. Further study of the intimate link between the Word and the Sacrament in the intervening years, especially at the French Liturgical Week in Strasbourg in 1957,[7] seems to minimize the "historical accident" of the fusion of the synagogal service (reading and praying) with the new mystery of the Breaking of the Bread. These studies show greater affinity between the two parts than was suspected by the preceding generations of pure historians. As Jesus was physically present at the Last Supper, so He is present in His Word during the Fore Mass. I still favor the vesting after the Gospel, but I can see good reasons for not changing the present rite in this matter — not only esthetic, but even pas-

[6] These are proposed for the opening of the Offertory, where the rudimentary Oremus is the last witness of this ancient tradition. The Oremus at the Offertory is not taken up by any Collect now, but is widely separated from the next Collect, the Secreta (to which it probably did not belong). It used to introduce what Bishop Carroll called a "prayer for Church and civil authorities."

[7] See *Parole de Dieu et liturgie, Le congrès de Strasbourg* (Paris: Cerf, 1958), especially the articles by A. M. Roguet, O.P., pp. 127 ff., and Pierre Jounel, pp. 17 ff.; English trans., *The Liturgy and the Word of God* (Collegeville, Minn.: Liturgical Press, 1959).

toral qualms. (The old "potato sack" alb in untidy folds, baggy and askew, is a heavy argument for a tidy chasuble. However, we are still perfectible and the mere necessity to present ourselves in public may take care of the esthetics . . .)

The Service of the Word

There is a great difference between the Entrance Rite and the Service of the Word. The first is all movement, singing and common prayer. But with the second, the congregation settles down to receive, to listen, to ponder and reflect, to be taught by the Word Himself in three, or at least two, readings from Holy Scripture. First, as we hope, there will be a Lesson from the Old Testament, as a background and prophecy; second (or first) the apostles will speak to us, making a path for: last, the Word Himself, in the Gospel which makes Christ present in the Church.

The Gradual is a response sung by the choir or cantors as a reflective "mood" piece; the Alleluia or Tract is a shout of welcome to the spiritual presence of Christ in His Word. This Word is followed by the appropriate explanation in a homily or sermon. Now the congregation is ready to hear about the affairs of their own communal life (announcements, etc.), to confess their faults and to pray for the intentions of the Church, world-wide and local, in the so-called "Bidding Prayers" or Litanies.

There is an ascending line of word-architecture from the Lesson to the Gospel. In this ascent to Christ, souls are disposed for cleansing and for intercession for one another.

7. *Old Testament Lesson.* Since there seems to be general agreement that more Scripture should be read during the year, this seems to me the place to revive the reading of a third Scripture lesson, only, however, where there is sufficient time available. The Gradual might be divided for use after both the Lesson and the Epistle, or set between the restored Lesson and the present Epistle. In the latter case, the Alleluia or Tract would then fill the interval between the Epistle and Gospel.

Everything takes place in the sanctuary (in choro) unless otherwise indicated.

	Solemn Mass	Chanted Mass	Recited Mass	Devotional Mass
7. Old Testament Lesson and*/or Epistle (all sit) read at lectern facing people* No Deo gratias*	subdeacon (or lector*)	lector*	do.*	cel.
8. Gradual, Alleluia, Tract, Sequence	choir	do.	chorus*	cel.
9. Munda cor, etc. Silent blessing	deacon cel.	cel. do.	do. do.	do. do.
10. Gospel responses Gospel at ambo/pulpit* No response at the end*	all* deacon only*	do.* cel.	do.* do.	server do.
11. Homily	cel. (or deacon*)	cel.	do.	do.
12. Announcements	cel. (or deacon*)	cel.	do.	omit
Bidding Prayers*	cel. (or deacon) & cong.*	cel. & cong.*	do.*	cel. & server*
Confession*	cel. (or deacon) & cong.*	cel. & cong.*	do.*	cel. & server*

*Features that are either new, in a new setting or derived from principles ruling OHSI.

_____SCHEMA II_____

Fifty-two Sunday Lessons, plus the feasts of obligation (multiplied by three or four in case a three- or four-year course of readings [8] is accepted), would cover the Old Testament rather comprehensively.

8. *The Responsory Songs — Gradual, Alleluia, Tract, Sequence.* This group of songs has a double purpose: To express a meditative response to the reading just heard and to serve as

---

[8] On this subject, see H. Schuermann, "Une répartition triennale des péricopes pour les dimanches et jours de fête," P&L, 39 (1957), 230 ff., and Hofinger *et al., Worship, the Life of the Missions* (Notre Dame University Press, 1958), pp. 84 ff.

a climactic preparation for the next reading, e.g., the Alleluia is a burst of jubilation welcoming the "Word" of the Gospel. They are elaborate compositions, both in their chant setting and in polyphony, and cannot, therefore, be sung congregationally. I think this is all to the good: a reflective mood should now settle over the congregation as being now an *audience*, definitely receptive during the Service of the Word. Here they should be given "a break" in constant response and activity (quite apart from the fact that some phase of the service should be allotted to good music as such).

Where a good schola is not available and the danger of mediocre or poor music exists, there is still the possibility of using a soloist, or psalmodic singing or recitation by a chorus, or of a choral hymn, which of course should conform to the minimal requirements for such hymns as expressed in the Instruction: It should be good musically; in content it should express the thoughts and moods of the displaced texts; and it should be in the spirit of the season if not of the very texts which are read on this occasion.

9. The Devotional Prayers of the Sacred Ministers — Munda cor, etc. If retained at all, it is obvious that they should never interfere with the progress of the action; since the responsorial songs are being performed while the proper ministers prepare for the solemn announcement of God's Word, these prayers should be recited inaudibly, or at least so as not to interfere with the singing.

10. The Gospel. Great solemnity ought to make the "Presence of Christ in His Word and as the Word" the climax of this part of the Mass. The procession with the Gospel Book,[9] with candles and incense (at all types of rites except the "devotional Mass"), and accompanied by the Alleluia, should be impressive. The minister is the deacon or the celebrant as now. The Gospel should be sung or read clearly from the ambo. (It has been suggested that the Gospel Book should always

[9] The Gospel Book should, by its outward appearance, indicate clearly its dignity as the vehicle of the Word.

rest on the altar before the tabernacle, and be taken from the altar before the chanting of the Gospel, the *kerygma*.) I agree with Father Jungmann that the responses at the end of both readings (Deo gratias; Laus tibi, Christe), unless sung or recited by the immediate assistants, will never come out in unison and should therefore better be dropped altogether. They are late additions and, although corresponding acclamations exist in the Armenian and Byzantine rites, their assignment to the servers and the fact that they are not sung in our present rite, classify them as being word accompaniments of late-medieval vintage. Unless they are to be done solemnly, they should be eliminated altogether.

11. The Breaking of the Spiritual Bread — The Sermon or Homily. The sermon should be relocated immediately after the ending of the Gospel (before the announcements etc.), to manifest the fact that it is a part of the *kerygma* and springs from the Word of God. Announcements should *follow* the sermon.

I wish to make a strong argument to the effect that there should be no extraneous matter between the Gospel and its explanation. The latter is a part of the sacred liturgy, a continuation of the Word of God, a part of the heralding (*kerygma*) of the salvation of mankind through the Word become Flesh, not a catechetical instruction, a pep talk or a meditation on a pious subject of the preacher's own choice. It should be given from the sanctuary (altar or ambo); it must come from the same area from which the Sacrament takes its origin.

12. The Announcements, Bidding Prayers and Confession. After the (short) announcements is the place for prayer in common for special intentions: the so-called Litanies or Bidding Prayers.[10] The Dominus vobiscum and Oremus, at the beginning of the Offertory, which now "float in space," detached from any prayer, are ready-made to open these litanies. This would relocate the Credo as an introduction to the Sacrifice: at present it follows an intellectual pattern as being a response to indoctrination. If, instead, it opens the Anaphora, it will again have

[10] See P&L, 39 (1957), pp. 176 ff.

the sacramental character it possesses in the baptismal rite, and once possessed more evidently in the Mass. It will then again be part of the mystery, not a school-room rehearsal of knowledge.

The order would then be as follows: First, the parish announcements — mostly references to a parish bulletin, to save time and avoid trivialities. Second, the Bidding Prayers or Litanies. Third, the open confession: a shorter Confiteor and general absolution.

The Bidding Prayers. Professor Balthasar Fischer of the Trier Seminary has concentrated much of his learned effort on this part of the liturgy. In *Liturgisches Jahrbuch* (Münster: Aschendorff, 1951), he published an exhaustive study of this ancient prayer for insertion in the services of popular Vespers and Lauds. For the new diocesan prayerbook for the Diocese of Trier (p. 517), he also composed litanies to be recited by priest and people in alternation after the "service of the Word," that is, after the residual Oremus that now incongruously adorns the beginning of the Offertory. Here he varies the prayers in content according to the season of the year, not according to the topics prescribed by the needs of the parish and the *imperata* of the Ordinary. To combine both would make for a variation that would break the otherwise inevitable monotony and still leave room for the "folk-near" (to render a favorite German term) causes and needs of the people present. This litany-form is true popular prayer, as Father Jungmann's careful study of liturgical worship has sufficiently proved. The following is an attempt to reproduce Father Fischer's work, the first seven prayers being the "proper" for Passiontide.

> Let us Pray:
> Lord Jesus Christ, Son of the living God, obedient to the will of the Father unto death on the cross.
>
> *All*: Have mercy on us.
> *Cel.*: Man of sorrows, afflicted because of our sins,
> *All*: Have mercy on us.
> *Cel.*: Lamb of God, who takest away the sins of the world,
> *All*: Have mercy on us.

Cel.: That, by Thy blood, Thou mayest cleanse Thy people of all their defilement,

All: We beseech Thee, hear us.

Cel.: That, for the sake of Thy precious blood, Thou wouldst not cast away us sinners,

All: We beseech Thee, hear us.

Cel.: That, through the power of Thy Holy Passion, Thou wouldst strengthen and glorify all who are persecuted for Thy name's sake,

All: We beseech Thee, hear us.

Cel.: That Thy Holy Cross may unlock the gates of paradise to the souls of all deceased in Thy name,

All: We beseech Thee, hear us.

Cel.: For our Holy Father Pope (*N.*), our bishops and the priests, let us pray.

All: Lord, have mercy on them.

Cel.: For our government and all who serve us in public office, let us pray.

All: Lord, have mercy on them.

Cel.: For all who serve the people of God in the religious state, let us pray.

All: Lord, have mercy on them.

Cel.: For our children, young people, and their educators, let us pray.

All: Lord, have mercy on them.

Cel.: For those who have chosen the married state and parenthood, let us pray.

All: Lord, have mercy on them.

Cel.: For all who are troubled in mind and body, for the poor, the sick, the dying, and the persecuted, let us pray.

All: Lord, have mercy on them.

Cel.: For our benefactors and friends, as well as our enemies and persecutors, let us pray.

All: Lord, have mercy on them.

Cel.: For the special intentions *NN.* and *NN.*, let us pray.

All: Lord, have mercy (*or*) We beseech Thee, hear us.

Cel.: For Thou, O Lord, hast given Thy life as a ransom for the sins of the world, Thou has purchased us by Thy death on the cross: we praise Thee and glorify Thee with the Father and the Holy Spirit in Thy holy Church. To Thee be honor and glory through all ages to come.

All: Amen.

Cel.: Let us confess our sins,[11]

All: We confess to Almighty God, to Blessed Mary ever Virgin, to the Blessed Angels, the Apostles, the Martyrs, and all the Saints, to the whole Church and to you, Father, that we have sinned in thought, word and deed: through what we have done and what we have left undone. We therefore pray for forgiveness through our Lord and Saviour, Jesus Christ.

Cel.: May Almighty God forgive you your sins and lead you to life everlasting.

All: Amen.

[11] Our present Confiteor is repetitious and too long. There was a common agreement with Father Jungmann at the Lugano Conference that a shorter form is needed, perhaps modelled after that of one of the other Western liturgies.

III Contemplated Reforms in the Anaphora

Offertory Rites and Prayers

An Offertory rite, simpler and less grandiose than the present "little Canon," [1] is needed to bring out the true function of this preparation of the elements and persons for the real Canon. After the washing of hands and the putting on of full vestments, the host and chalice are made ready on the credence table. This is a simple enough prerequisite for the Banquet-Sacrifice to follow. As soon as the two processions with the gifts begin — one of the clergy with host and wine, the other of the congregation with hosts and donations — the great Offertory chant is alternated between the schola and the offering congregation; the altar is incensed as also are the ministers and people; the great Collect, "Super oblata," is sung and the faithful respond, "Amen."

Schema III shears away the superabundance of late medieval additions and brings out the essentials: the readying of both persons and elements in simple, self-explanatory form. All the wordy, slightly misleading and extraneous prayers which are not essential are done away with, especially the suggestion that we have a bread and wine sacrifice within the mystery-sacrament of the Sacrifice of Christ. All is now ready for the True Sacrifice.

The changes indicated here are so great because the present

[1] On the "Little Canon" as a name for the Offertory, see Maertens in P&L, 39 (1957), 296 ff., and Jungmann, *Missa Sollemnis*, II, 78.

	Solemn Mass	Chanted Mass	Recited Mass	Devotional Mass
13. Credo	cel. intones; choir & cong. alternate	do.	cel. intones; lector* and cong. alternate	cel.
	cel. washes hands at credence table,* omitting Psalm*	do.	do.	cel. washes hands at altar, omitting Psalm*
	sacred min. vest in chasuble, tunic, etc. at credence table	cel. vests in chasuble and maniple at credence table	do.	omit
14. Preparation of Gifts	cel. & deacon at credence table*	cel. at credence table*	do.*	cel. at altar
Suscipe, Sancte Pater	cel.	cel.	cel.	cel.
Deus, qui humanae	omit*	do.*	do.*	do.*
Offerimus*	cel.	cel.	cel.	cel.
In spiritu humilitatis	omit*	do.*	do.*	do.*
Veni, sanctificator	omit*	do.*	do.*	do.*
Suscipe, Sancta Trinitas	omit*	do.*	do.*	do.*
15. Offertory Antiphon and Verses (begun as soon as Credo is finished*)	choir & cong.*	do.*	leader & cong.*	omit
16. Offertory Processions[2]	sacred min. & lay reps.*	cel. & lay reps.*	do.*	omit
17. Orate, fratres	cel.	do.	do.	do.
Suscipiat	omit*	do.*	do.*	do.*
18. Secret (aloud*)	cel.	do.	do.	do.
19. Amen.*	all	do.	do.	server

*Indicates a change of rite, text or place, or an omission.

_____SCHEMA III_____

Offertory is now overloaded with symbolism and wordy prayers of doubtful value, and therefore needs simplification and pastoral development as well as liturgical pruning of wild growth.

[2] *Liturgisches Jahrbuch*, 8 (Trier, 1958), 243 ff.

It cannot be emphasized too much that the Offertory is not an anticipated Canon nor a sacrifice of natural gifts, for this would be a relapse into the Old Testament sacrifice and a denial of the oneness of Christ's sacrifice. The Offertory is, rather, a "making ready" of minds and of the elements of the Sacrament.

13. The Credo. The celebrant intones it at the bench; the choir and congregation alternate thereafter unto the end. *14.* While this is being done, the celebrant washes his hands — without the psalm. (The present Lavabo presupposes the old handling of offertory gifts in kind. Its psalm, added in the late medieval period, shows the tendency of that time to accompany even the most obvious gesture with wordy recitations. The references to an "unholy folk" and "bribes" are not so immediately obvious to our faithful as to make adequate sense — even if the psalm were audible. Since it originally pertained to private devotion, and is recited *pro forma* and in a great hurry by present-day clerics, it might as well be abolished.)

After the Lavabo, the sacred ministers vest in maniple and outer vestments.[3]

Then the host and chalice are prepared by the sacred ministers, using only the two remaining and shortened prayer formulas. (See the sample Mass, p. 85.)

15. The Offertory Processional[4] *and, 16. The Offertory*

[3] In the case of the deacon, the vesting at this point is the opposite of the current ritual, according to which at this point during Advent and Lent he takes off the *planeta plicata* and dons the *stola lata*. However the latter is now an empty ceremony: the *stola lata* is really a rolled up *planeta plicata*, once a bulky affair that reached all the way down below the wrists. It had to be got out of the way to give the then-very-active deacon freedom of action for his hands and arms. That it is purely ceremonial now is obvious: The broad stole is entirely different from the folded large chasuble and the deacon has little to do requiring use of his arms which cannot be done decorously wearing a tunic or a folded chasuble. I make this note only to reassure the readers that I am conscious of the *reversal*. We have here a true case of practical "archaism" lasting long after its true meaning has been lost.

[4] This, like the responsorial songs after the Epistle, is an elaborate piece of verbal and musical composition, especially in its fuller form (viz., Dom Hesbert's *Antiphonale sextuplex* [Brussels, 1938]. Either a soloist, a few cantors, or a well-trained choir should sing the body of the Antiphon, now called the *Offertorium* or, in the OHSI, *Antiphona ad Offertorium.* The refrain verse should be psalmodic and easily sung by a congregation. After the cantors repeat the body of the Antiphon, the short refrain is sung, the Antiphon is repeated, and so on, until the time has come for the celebrant's (Orate fratres

Procession. After the Credo, the gifts are prepared on the credence table, and are carried in a smaller procession to the altar (celebrant and deacon) while the subdeacon (or deacon) in solemn Masses, an acolyte in other Masses, accepts the people's donations at the altar rail, where they have been brought by lay people representing the congregation. Both processions should be accompanied by the singing of the "Antiphon of the Offertory" and its verses. At solemn Masses, the gifts and the altar, as well as the clergy and people are to receive incensation; the altar and gifts by the celebrant, the others by the deacon or incense-bearer.

17. The Orate Fratres. I propose that this either be suppressed, as it is not, even at present, part of the singing at Mass and is really directed to the clergy, not to the people;[5] or, since it has been raised in significance by the OHSI, that it be used to introduce the Secret, leaving out the Suscipiat.

18. The Oratio super oblata or Secret. This is a genuine Offertory prayer.[6] Not even the word "Secreta" means "secret-silent," but "secreta (secernere) — set apart," i.e., the prayer over the gifts selected, set apart, for the Sacrifice-Banquet. It ought to be sung in the tone of a Collect, following the singing of the Offertory Antiphon and Verses.

19. The Concluding Amen of the Congregation. This, like the Amen after the Collect, after the Bidding Prayers, after the coming Great Doxology and after the Last Blessing, is one of the

---

and) Collect over the gifts (Super oblata-Secreta). The Instruction would allow a hymn in the vernacular during this time in a dialog Mass. I hope this permission will be extended to sung Masses in future reforms, with one condition however: that we first ransack the available texts and melodies and see that the hymns at least strive to equal the magnificent treasure of the existing Offertoria plus verses. After developing the Gelineau Psalms and improving them musically, some such substitute for the present wealth in Latin could be tried out. On solemn occasions, the archives of our polyphonic masters should be scanned for existing or adaptable music, again alternated with short responsorial verses sung by the congregation. The case is different from that of the Gradual, etc., because here the people are actively engaged, not passive listeners to be inspired to meditation. This seems to me a very significant difference; and it shows the variety which we should keep in mind. Nothing can be cut over the same last, everything deserves individual attention.

[5] See Maertens, P&L, 39 (1957), 167.
[6] See Maertens, P&L, 40 (1958), 120 ff.

testimonies of participation, which should never be denied to the people. There should be a noticeable pause between it and the start of the Preface-Canon, of which it is not a part — although it seems to be merely an introductory versicle in our present rite.

The Sacred Canon

Silent or chanted? Scholars agree that the Canon was sung or chanted until the eighth or ninth century, when there was a radical change of emphasis. The mementos or diptichs were probably recited by the deacon rather than by the celebrant. It is declaredly not the intention of the Holy See to resurrect archaic usages, but rather to be guided by tradition in search of the best pastoral aptness of the liturgy. Both principles are important: the welfare of the souls which inspires the whole reform, and guidance by sound tradition. In most cases, this tradition will be that practice which is closest in time to the composition of the texts and rites. These will be maintained with as little change as the pastoral principle permits.[7] An audible Canon, therefore, is justified on the grounds of tradition. And there seems to be general agreement that such a Canon, whether chanted, sung, or recited, would lead to better participation, if carried out with devotion and care. Since the intercessory prayers (litanies) have already taken care of the mementos as far as the congregation is concerned, it would apparently be advisable to let the celebrant recite them without naming any particular names. The Canon should then be chanted in the same tone of voice, from the beginning of the Preface to the Great Doxology. This Doxology would be sung or recited in a more solemn and elaborate melody. Since this is a radical departure from the more recent tradition, and since a certain timidity in these matters now prevails in the minds of the majority, this restoration is suggested only as an example of thorough reform.

[7] See Maertens on the history of the Canon in the service of pastoral theology in P&L, 39 (1957), 279–305. Companion articles of the Offertory (P&L, 40 [1958], 114–136) and Communion (*Ibid.*, pp. 345–359) have since appeared.

It is obvious that all the responses to the initial salutations of the Preface are given by the congregation (OHSI & Instruction). The Canon *begins* with these salutations, and not after the Sanctus. The Sanctus is recited or sung, without division, through the Benedictus, by celebrant, ministers, schola, and the whole congregation. Even in the event that a silent Canon is retained, the celebrant ought to wait until the end of the Sanctus before starting the Te igitur, as a simple matter of consistency in the effort to let the people participate in his action and words.[8]

The congregation should stand throughout the Canon, and genuflect only between the two warning bells, while the words of the Consecration are being pronounced. It would be appropriate if the faithful made a profound inclination after seeing the Blessed Sacrament raised at the Great Doxology — i.e., at the end of the Canon during the singing of the Doxology.

A look at this schema shows a few of the changes in the rite — concerning the tone of voice, the ringing of bells, the postures, and the elevations — which are all inspired by pastoral considerations. They would clarify the rite and prevent its being mistaken for a mere incomprehensible ritual, with the emphasis in the wrong places.

Proposed Changes in the Text of the Canon. Many authors have referred to the multiplication of conclusions and Amens that interrupt the flow of the continuous text. Hippolytus of Rome and St. Ambrose (in *De sacramentis*) have an apparently older and more flowing version of the Canon, with no interrupting Amens. No one wants to replace the venerable present Canon, but it is suggested that it be freed from its accrescences. (See Lugano report.)

There is one addition to the Memento vivorum: the *"pro qui-*

[8] The bell at the Sanctus is definitely not a warning bell to be rung before the Sanctus, but a joyous accompaniment to the words and music of the Sanctus itself. Cf. the analogous practice in the Gloria of Maundy Thursday and during the Paschal Vigil. The bell should be used as a warning only before and after the actual words of consecration. These three, then, would be the only uses of bells during the Canon. The Cistercian rite is the model here. At a minimum, the senseless ringing of bells during the genuflections of the celebrant should be discontinued.

The entire canon is audible. Certain indicated prayers are sung or recited in a loud voice.

		Remarks
Dominus vobiscum	cel.	
Et cum spiritu tuo	all	and so forth, for the other versicles preceding the Preface
Preface	cel.	sung or recited in a loud voice
Sanctus (complete*)	intoned by schola*	concluded by all, in a loud voice, including cel. and sacred min.*
Te igitur	cel.	only one sign of the cross*
Memento	cel.	omit "pro quibus tibi offerimus"*
Communicantes	cel.	omit "Andreae" to "Damiani"*
Hanc igitur	cel.	omit "Per Christum, etc."*
Quam oblationem	cel.	sign of the cross at "benedictam," "Corpus," and "Sanguis" only*
Words of institution	cel.	omit double elevation,* or, if retained, ring bell only once,* at the actual elevations
Unde et	cel.	omit signs of the cross*
Supra quae	cel.	
Supplices te	cel.	omit "Per eundem Christum, etc."*
Memento etiam	cel.	omit "Per eundem Christum, etc."; bow of head transferred*
Nobis quoque	cel.	omit "Mathia" to "Anastasia" *
Per quem	cel.	only one large sign of the cross*
Per ipsum	cel.	sung aloud; all crosses are omitted; and the Blessed Sacrament is elevated high enough to be seen by all*
Amen	all	modo solemniore*

*Indicates a change from the present rite.

The reduction of words and in the number of signs of the cross and so forth will help in the avoidance of unseemly haste and misinterpretation and will eliminate certain later and unnecessary additions to the rite.[9] On the transfer of the solemn elevation to the Great Doxology, its former and more logical location, see below, pp. 68-69.

————————————————————————SCHEMA IV————

bus tibi offerimus" — dating from the Frankish period — which seems to exclude the direct participation of the congregation. This is "recent," and could be abolished without loss. As a matter of fact, the context gains through this excision of foreign matter.

[9] On the shortening of the prayers of the Canon, see the report of an address

The conclusions, as shown in our schema, of the Hanc igitur, Supplices te, and the Memento etiam [10] are all omitted. Thus, full impact is given to the solemn Amen at the end of the Canon. The text again becomes remarkably flowing, and much of the talk about its being an incongruous amalgam of disparate pieces will disappear.

The List of the Roman Saints. This may be regarded as a welcome contribution to the pastoral readjustments of the Canon. Both lists need and ought to be shortened. The full lists are onerous and, in view of the recent calendar reform, obsolete; many of the feasts in honor of these ancient saints have disappeared. They are a great inducement to parish priests to hurry or to slur; and, apart from the apostles, they are purely local personages who may be said to be of little or no visible significance to the universal Church. If, in the first list, at the Communicantes, only Rome (or Italy) were obliged to recite the names after Peter and Paul, with the rest of the Church omitting these names, the text would become fluent and pithy. At the Nobis quoque, the same omission could be made after Stephen, leaving John the Baptist and the first martyr as representatives of saints and martyrs, but omitting the long enumeration from Matthias to Anastasia. Here, too, the text would flow coherently

---

by Dom Paul Gordan of Beuron delivered in Vienna — carried in *Herder Korrespondenz,* 6 (1956), 269. The occasion was a pastoral meeting of the Austrian clergy in January of 1956. Dom Paul stressed "the impermeability and opaqueness of the present rite of the Mass, which was a stop-gap devised in 1570 under different cultural and scholarly conditions for the simple pastoral needs of the day; many parts are too long, as, e.g., the Prayers at the foot of the altar, the Offertory prayers. . . . In the Canon we have lists of saints dictated by considerations of an earlier century and the local preferences of a city; it contains superfluous signs of the cross and Amens, . . . [which] minimize the sweep from the Preface to the Doxology."

[10] The Memento mortuorum now ends *"Per Christum Dominum Nostrum, Amen,"* and, according to our present rubrics, the celebrant bows his head at the word "Christum," an unusual and never sufficiently explained action which is normally reserved to the Name, not the titles, of our Lord. Whatever its meaning and origin may have been, the bow becomes meaningful if we eliminate this conclusion, which is really no conclusion at all. The Memento would then conclude with the words ". . . *pacis ut indulgeas deprecamur,"* and would be immediately followed, with the bow and the striking of the breast, by *"Nobis quoque peccatoribus* . . ." In this way, the bowing of the head and the striking of the breast would be linked to the humble words, "To us also, thy sinful servants . . ." and would make admirable sense. Perhaps this is the way it was before the present "conclusion" was added.

without the roster of both obscure and famous saints far removed in history from modern man; in what way are they preferable to Francis, Teresa, and the other Ignatius? The pruned texts, as can easily be seen, make complete sense — more so than ever.

Transfer of the Elevation during the Canon.[11] The present double elevation, was, it appears, introduced for a reason that now seems quite dated. At the University of Paris,[12] in the thirteenth century, the learned theologians debated whether the consecration of the bread was complete after the words "This is my Body," or whether the two consecratory sentences were one whole and the consecration complete only after both sentences had been finished. The first school raised the Host for adoration after the (presumed) consecration of the Host only; the second school raised the Host and chalice together after both consecratory formulas had been spoken. When it was decided that the first school was the more correct according to scholastic thinking, the separate elevation after each consecration prevailed. The twofold elevation is therefore a remnant of a controversy long settled. Its retention is an illustration of a French proverb: "Ce n'est que le provisoire qui reste (What is of temporary value stubbornly stays on)."

On the other hand, these two elevations have had practical consequences that may have helped to obscure the clarity of the central part of the Mass: They have led to a secondary veneration of the Blessed Sacrament *within* the Canon. This is demonstrated by the singing of Corpus Christi hymns and motets between the elevations and the Pater noster, and the rich growth of private devotions inserted between the Consecration and the Pater noster which can be found in any book of so-called "Mass devotions." The worship of the Blessed Sacrament (here considered as *terminus ad quem*), valid as it is in view of heresy

[11] On the shift of emphasis to the Eucharist as the object of worship, see Maertens in P&L, 39 (1957), 298; R. P. Holyvet, "Présence divine et Eucharistie," P&L, 41 (1959), 181 ff. In the context of Communion, Maertens (P&L, 41 [1959], 355 ff.) discusses the "loss of symbolic understanding."
[12] According to Dumoutet, *Le désir de voir l'Hostie* (Paris, 1926).

and indifference, has its proper place *outside* the Mass. During Mass it may interfere with the proper attitudes, and create problems that adversely affect the attitude toward the Canon after the Consecration. We hope, therefore, that the practice of two elevations will eventually be discontinued and a return made to the thirteen hundred-year old procedure followed before the theological quarrel at the University of Paris. One elevation of the Blessed Sacrament under both species, surrounded by the splendor of the final Doxology, cannot but enhance the solemnity and true devotion to the Sacrament and the Mass. Some have argued in favor of the twin elevation of the late Middle Ages, that it has by now been surrounded with popular devotion and carries an element of "offering" in its gestures. The popular devotion cannot be denied; but the question is, whether it has not, in the long run, miscarried. The popular devotion concentrates uniquely on the Real Presence and veneration of the Species, a veneration which is thus taken out of its true place (at Corpus Christi and during other devotions) and is given this partial and isolating aspect. This attitude lacks the totality inherent in the full eucharistic worship of the Mass. In the Mass, the Holy Eucharist is the sacred and sublime *means* to the supreme end of worship. The element of offering, if it should be sought at all in a gesture, is present in the second and more ancient elevation — indeed, it is more present here, when the two species are elevated together: a true elevation of the whole Sacrament, with the "second" species raised to its presently rather neglected equality (in a liturgical sense, of course). By eliminating the twin elevations, the flow of the Canon would no longer be interrupted, the popular speculation about the enigmatic content of the prayers after the Consecration would come to an end, and the value of the Amen of the final Doxology would be restored.

There is at present little hope that this transfer of the solemn elevation and its reinstatement as one elevation, together with a solemn proclamation of its intent as worship of the Father through the Son in the Spirit, will be looked upon benignly by those who fear that such a return to a soberer aspect of this liturgy might be labeled "liturgical archaism" — so roundly and emphatically condemned in *Mediator Dei*. However, those who follow our argumentation without suspicion will notice that it was not inspired by reasons of a return to more ancient ways for the sake of more ancient forms; the argument went the other way — pastoral and liturgical reasons were the cause. Secondly, the obsolescence of the former reasoning in favor of a double elevation was noted, and only then was a remedy sought, under the guidance of an older and rudimentarily still-existing practice (for there *is* the so-called "little" elevation with its Doxology all ready made and extant).

As we said before, the elevations are the result of a very specialized controversy among theologians, and have become in the minds of the people gestures of a sacramental veneration which does not look on the Mass as a means to approach the Father through His Son, but as an act of worship which comes to rest and terminates in the Blessed Sacrament. This is legitimate worship, but it is adequately taken care of in the Feast of Corpus Christi, in exposition, in hours of adoration, and in processions.[13]

This confusion of the two attitudes has led to an estrangement of the common man, lay and clerical, from that participation which the texts require. Here is one of the reasons why the silence during the Canon is so readily and unquestioningly accepted: The Canon has become unimportant in the spiritual life of the last centuries.

I feel that, in view of the crippling effects — to use a strong term — of the latter attitude upon full worship by participation, this problem should be solved at its roots. This is the reason why

[13] *The* so-called *Instructio Clementina*, which regulates the devotion of the Forty Hours, makes a special issue out of its rule that no Mass should be celebrated at the altar of exposition unless it is absolutely necessary, and Pius XII specifically stated that the reason for this is that a clear and visible separation should be maintained between the one and the other form of eucharistic worship.

This is not the best place for adoration of the Son present in the Sacrament with special emphasis on the *vis naturalis concomitantiae*, terminating in the Sacrament and leaving the Father, so to speak, out of the field of vision.

I am discussing it at such length. It is not an archaism, nor a pet idea; it tries to heal a breach made in one of our most salutary traditions.

The elimination of the first two elevations will achieve two effects: the showing of the two species together would be re-established, and, with it, its great significance. And the Canon would flow more logically and uninterruptedly. I am not alone; this proposal is a very old one. We also know that the present arrangement has been defended by prominent and scholarly liturgists — as a gesture of offering, for instance — but I feel that this is a rationalization to spare the people, so as not to disturb their mental attitude. But isn't it just this attitude which stands in the way of a better understanding and more fruitful practice?

In order to forestall a debate that is beside the point, may I repeat that I realize that the present usage is hard to change; that the shock caused by a change, especially if unheralded, will be as great as that caused in some places by the new laws of fast, of evening Mass, and of the new Holy Week — perhaps even greater. But I do think that after calm dogmatic, pastoral, liturgical, and ascetic consideration, the elimination of the first double elevation and the restoration of the ancient and more traditional Great Doxology might be deemed the better way. I insert this lengthy disquisition here, true to my stated objective of giving the most *advanced* version of liturgical reform in order to make the whole issue clearer.[14] How this rite might be carried out is, of course, subject to the ruling of the official source of all reforms, the Sacred Congregation of Rites. The Doxology would begin with the words *"per ipsum et cum ipso et in ipso est tibi,* etc.," omitting the present signs of the cross made with hand and host and the preceding genuflection. While these solemn words were being chanted (or recited in Masses without

[14] I wish to add that most suggestions of reform demand at least the solemn (audible) Doxology, and that this is foreshadowed by the great emphasis given in *Mediator Dei* and in the Instruction to the Amen that follows. This is also maintained by those who have never proposed restoration of the "little" elevation to its pristine dignity and uniqueness.

choir), both species would be raised so that they could be seen by the ministers and the congregation, who then solemnly respond: Amen.

The Altar Kisses.[15] The kissing of the altar is still an eloquent gesture of loving veneration given sacred objects like the Bible (the flag and the sword in the secular realm); to kiss the altar at the Te igitur and the Supplices is so well established in tradition that these kisses should remain the two significant, and therefore the only, altar kisses outside the greeting kiss at the Introit and the farewell kiss before the Last Blessing. Jungmann (at Lugano) suggested that the multiplication of kisses be done away with.

The Signs of the Cross over the Altar and the Species. The signs of the cross need a serious reconsideration. Their multiplication is disturbing, esthetically undesirable, and in practice usually hurried. In some places they are mere stylized pointing gestures, when, for example, the celebrant mentions the Sacred Species. These "pointing crosses" should be distinguished from blessings. So long as a blessing gesture is involved, a single sign of the cross should be maintained, according to all who have expressed opinions on the subject. This means signs of the cross at the word *"Bene † dicas"* in the Te igitur, at *"bene † dictam"* in Quam oblationem, at *"bene † dixit"* in both consecratory formulas, and elimination of the sign of the cross in all other places in the Canon (see Schema IV), and certainly in all places outside the Canon, except where blessings are truly involved — incense, the deacon and the subdeacon, the Last Blessing, etc.

[15] J. Hofinger, in *Worship: The Life of the Missions* (Notre Dame University Press, 1958), suggests that Oriental peoples for whom kissing is *not* a gesture of respect, and to whom its use in the liturgy seems strange and even disgusting, might be allowed to omit all kisses from the rites.

IV Contemplated Reforms in the Communion Rite

Reforms in the Communion Rite

The Communion Service should be revised in a thorough fashion. The Lord's Prayer, as the ancient preparation for Communion, should set the scheme of things. The Kiss of Peace follows as the spiritual preparation; then, the physical preparation, the breaking of the Host, accompanied by the traditional Agnus Dei. The proximate preparation, the "personal" prayers of devotion, would be left to the discretion of the celebrant. The actual Communion Rite would be accompanied by the singing of the Communion Antiphon and Psalms by the schola and the people, while the celebrant (or deacon) would say only, to the individual communicant, "Corpus Christi," to which the communicant would respond "Amen."

The Postcommunion part would remain unchanged, except that the Placeat would be omitted and in place of the duplicated Gospel (the so-called "last" Gospel) there will be a recessional such as hymn or a Marian antiphon (as the procession goes past our Lady's shrine).

This schema does not indicate the possible introduction of some brief canticle or psalm after Communion to make the conclusion of Mass seem less abrupt. The form such a rite should take is problematical. Perhaps the simplest solution would be an extension of the Communion psalmody and antiphon, concluded by the (one) Postcommunion prayer, followed by dismissal and blessing. In any event, such a "thanksgiving"

The present schema first of all numbers the parts of the present Communion service, so that it might more easily illustrate the omissions and rearrangements in the restored service. Please note that the responses in the restored service are assigned to proper groups.

1. Pater noster	cel.	1. Pater noster	cel. & cong.
2. Sed libera nos	ch./serv.		
2a. Amen	cel.		
3. Libera nos quaesumus	cel. (low voice)	3. Libera nos quaesumus	cel. (aloud)
4. Rite with empty paten	cel.		
5. Breaking host	cel.		
6. Per omnia saecula	cel.	6. Per omnia saecula	cel.
7a. Pax Domini (etc.)	cel.	6a. Amen	all
7b. Drop particle (Commixtio)	cel.	11. Domine Jesu Christe, qui dixisti	cel. & deac.
8. Et cum spiritu tuo	choir	7a. Pax Domini (etc.)	cel.
9. Haec commixtio	cel.	8. Et cum spiritu tuo	all
10. Agnus Dei	cel./ch.	12. Kiss of Peace	cel./deac./all(?)
11. Domine Jesu Christe, qui dixisti	cel./deac.	10. Agnus Dei	ch. & cong.
12. Kiss of Peace	cel. & min.	5. Beaking Host (During Agnus Dei)	cel.
13. Domine Jesu Christe . . . voluntate	cel.	13. Domine Jesu Christe . . . voluntate	cel. (facultative)
14. Perceptio (etc.)	cel.	14. Perceptio (etc.)	cel. (facultative)
14a. Domine, non sum	cel.	14a. Domine, non sum	cel. (omit bells)
15. Confiteor	subd./serv.		
16. Absolutions	cel.		
17. Ecce, Agnus Dei	cel.	17. Ecce, Agnus Dei	cel.
17a. Domine, non sum	cel.	17a. Domine, non sum	all
		20. Communion antiphon and psalms	ch. & cong.
18. Corpus Domini nostri	cel.	18. Corpus Christi	cel. (or deac.)
		18a. Amen	communicant
19. Remaining rites and prayers	cel., min./serv.	19. Remaining rites and prayers	cel., min,/serv.
20. Communion antiphon	cel./ch.		
21. Dominus vobiscum	cel.	21. Dominus vobiscum	cel.
22. Et cum spiritu tuo	ch./serv.	22. Et cum spiritu tuo	all
23. Oremus (Postcommunion prayer)	cel.	23. Oremus (Postcommunion prayer)	cel. (with pause after Oremus)
24. Amen	ch./serv.	24. Amen	all
25. Dominus vobiscum	cel.	25. Dominus vobiscum	cel.
25a. Et cum spiritu tuo	ch.	25a. Et cum spiritu tuo	all

26. Ite/Benedicamus	deac./cel.	26. Ite/Benedicamus	deac./cel.
27. Deo gratias	ch./serv.	27. Deo gratias	all
28. Placeat	cel.		
29. Blessing	cel.	29. Blessing	cel.
30. Response	serv.	30. Response	all
31. Last Gospel	cel.		
32. Deo gratias	serv.	32a. Recessional	all

_____SCHEMA V_____

should not follow the Postcommunion, and even less the Last Blessing.

This restoration omits the almost inexplicable rite with the empty paten; the "commixtion" or "immixtion" — equally hard to justify; the ringing of the bell at the celebrant's Communion (to which there is no good reason to draw attention, now that the people's Communion has attained the solemnity it deserves); the Placeat; and the anticlimactic repetition of a Gospel which is too weighty to be read as a time-filler, too important in its content to be merely recited, and tiring in its daily repetition.[1]

The Individual Changes. The new Good Friday service and the Instruction seem to indicate that there is a chance of having the Pater noster sung by the whole congregation. This would eliminate the Amen at the end. The celebrant would continue alone with the Libera nos in a loud voice, chanting it at a sung Mass.

The rearrangement of the ceremonies and the elimination of some of the hard-to-explain rites follows the work of Father Jungmann and other authorities. The signing with the empty paten during the Libera nos quaesumus is eliminated. The "Pax prayer," Domine Jesu Christe qui dixisti (11), follows the Amen of the Libera. The Pax is given at all Masses (12); it is given to the people *per instrumentum pacis,* i.e., through a cross

[1] Maertens, P&L, 1958, 5, p. 358, refers us to the medieval addiction to the "Initia" of the Gospels. The Last Gospel was not regarded as a part of the Mass during the Middle Ages. It was first used by the Dominicans. Besides being anticlimactic after the Service of the Word, it has the additional disadvantage of being inaudible at High Mass.

74   REFORMS IN THE

or "Pax Tablet" that is passed among them.[2] The Pax Domini itself (7a) is sung before the Kiss is given, after the celebrant has recited the Pax prayer (and kissed the altar). The Agnus Dei invocation is then made by the schola while the congregation makes the response (10). During the singing of the Agnus Dei, the celebrant breaks the Host. One large particle is reserved for his own Communion, the other for the Communion of the sacred ministers or servers.[3]

[2] The Pax Tablet or Pax Brede is a small sacred image of precious metal or some other material, the kissing of which substitutes for the Kiss of Peace. See Lercaro-O'Connell, *A Small Liturgical Dictionary* (London: Burns, Oates, 1959), pp. 193 ff.; Fattinger, *Liturgisch-Praktische Requisiten Kunde* (Freiburg: Herder, 1954), pp. 205 f.

[3] Maertens in P&L, 41, (1959), 345 ff., proves with great care and lucidity that far more would have to be done, than is here and in other places proposed, for a thorough reform:

1. The present breaking of the Host is not the direct descendant of the liturgical *Fractio panis* of the Last Supper and the early centuries, but is rather the offspring of a "minor and private" breaking of the pope's Host for use as *fermentum* to be sent to parish priests in Rome for Masses in their own churches to symbolize the oneness of their sacrifice with their bishop's. This very fact presumes a late date for the practice, i.e., when parishes had already developed.

2. The "commixtio et consecratio" of the ceremony refers to the "consecration by contact" of the ministerial chalices used for distribution of Holy Communion (a fraction of the consecrated Host and a few drops of the wine were "inmixed" in large chalices containing unconsecrated elements for distribution). The dropping of a particle of the celebrant's own Host into the chalice followed a new and allegorical development that has been described by De Jong (ALW [1953], pp. 78 ff. and the following vols.): the action symbolized [sic] the reunion of Body and Blood of the living Lord who had previously been in the symbolical state of a slain victim. This is, of course, dogmatically tortured and of a later age.

3. The original *fractio panis* in order to distribute the bread for Communion truly symbolizes (not allegorizes) only one thing: the participation in the one bread by the many; the oneness with the one victim, the one priest and the one Body of the Church; the essence of Communion, fully sufficient in itself. Allegorizing was responsible for the interpretation of the "breaking" of the Host as a token of the Passion and death, and for the connection with the "Lamb," which connection came from the East in the train of one of the Eastern pontiffs (the elaborate Offertory slaying in most of the Eastern rites speaks of one part of the host as Amnos, i.e., Lamb).

Dom Maertens proposes a thorough reform, and is hopeful that it will be made according to the dogmatically defensible symbolism of biblical origin. He hopes that a half-way measure will not result. How to bring about the reform without the reintroduction of large size hosts (leavened bread?), and eventually of Communion under both species, is hard to say. Even if the Holy See did intend to bring about such a reform eventually, there would still have to be a stage intermediate to the goal and the present state and that would be much as we have outlined in the text. A thorough-going reform would mean the elimination of the *fermentum,* whether the bishop's or — the later development — that of the previous day, the commixtion and the linking up

In this arrangement, the two prayers before the celebrant's Communion are made optional.[4] The celebrant takes up that part of the Host reserved for himself with the words "Panem caelestem accipiam." He then says privately the Domine, non sum dignus, without accompanying bell. After the celebrant's Communion, he gives the remainder of the large Host to the servers or sacred ministers at the altar. The normal assumption is that the Hosts required for the Mass have been consecrated at that Mass in a ciborium or on a special paten. The celebrant shows the Host with the words: "Ecce, Agnus Dei," etc., and the communicants join him in the Domine, non sum dignus.

As soon as the distribution of the Hosts is begun, the schola intones the Communion Antiphon, which is repeated by the congregation. Then the schola sings two Psalm verses and the congregation repeats the Antiphon as before. At recited Masses, these verses are said by a lector, who alternates with the people in the same fashion. If this procedure is not possible, an appropriate hymn is sung while the distribution of Communion is continued.

For the rest, the reforming of this final section of the Mass consists in the elimination of superfluities and the pruning away of additions that lead to a misunderstanding of the rite.

The use of Ite Missa est or Benedicamus Domino will no longer be ruled by the presence or absence of the Gloria in the Fore Mass; rather, as is logical, the use will depend upon whether the people are to leave the Church or are invited to remain for services that will follow (cf. OHSI for Holy Thursday).

The Placeat will be omitted. It is not Roman, but Gallican in origin. The Roman Mass does not address the Blessed Trinity, but the Father through the Son. (This is in line with the Mass itself, as we may note here, which is dynamically Trinitarian,

---

of the *fractio* with the Agnus Dei. That this also means the elimination of the "consecration by contact" will occasion no tears. Dom Maertens believes that the breaking of the Host for the people's Communion, a point to be made clear, is so obviously closely linked with the Kiss of Peace that it is beyond dispute.

[4] The private character of these prayers is emphasized in the diocesan directories mentioned by Dom Maertens in P&L, 1957, 3, 167.

not statically extra-Trinitarian: the Sacrifice is offered by Christ and the Church to the Father.)

The Last Blessing is the final rite of the Mass. The priest then leaves the altar. It is fitting that the congregation sing a recessional hymn.

This section of the Mass that we have been discussing is meant to prepare for and give Communion in a dogmatically sober, correct, and yet heart-warming spirit. Strong emphasis must be given to the communal aspect, the "Church-building" dynamics of the Sacrament of the Last Supper, which individualism and self-styled mysticism had almost obliterated beyond recognition. So many of our contemporary appeals for attendance at Mass and reception of Holy Communion seem to sail under "false colors." We try to "sell" our people on receiving Communion for this or that purpose, to further this or that devotion, as part of this or that practice, to yield this or that favor. But seldom do we encourage Communion for the one truly correct reason: to build the Church in ourselves and our parishes, i.e., Communion for Communion's sake. The reform of the Communion Service will clarify its purpose; hence the emphasis on the Our Father, the Kiss of Peace, the Breaking of the Host, the Hosts being consecrated at the Mass in which they are used (to employ a household expression that sounds trivial but carries meaning, "Feed them from the table, not from the larder"), the singing of Psalms during the Communion procession, the pruning away of all those rites which confuse, even when they are consistently and repeatedly explained.

V Sample Mass

A Revised Ordinarium Missae with an Adapted Proper of the Third Sunday after Pentecost

This Mass has been chosen because of its simplicity and appealing text.[1] Following the example of OHSI, I have numbered every part for reference. For the translations used, see Appendix C, p. 109.

Entrance Rite

1. *After vesting in the sacristy, the clergy proceed to the baptistery. The celebrant wears a cope. The other ministers wear albs and the deacon a stole (no maniples). At the gate of the baptistery the procession halts, and the deacon (at solemn Mass, otherwise the celebrant himself) dips the aspergile into the water container in its special place, turns to the assistants and congregation and sprinkles them, saying nothing.*

2. *The procession re-forms — subdeacon or acolyte carrying the cross; six, four or two acolytes carrying lighted candles; incense-bearer; book-bearers; subdeacon or deacon carrying Gospel Book; celebrant in cope — and moves with measured step to the altar.*

3. *Meanwhile, as soon as the clergy leave the sacristy, the choir intones the Entrance Processional. (Ps. 24:16, 18). This is followed by the Psalm,[2] alternating between the cantor and the congregation.*

---

[1] Also because it is one of the two Propers in Pentecost time which were not disrupted when, in the early Middle Ages, the texts for the Fourth Sunday were moved at least in part to the place of the First Sunday, and the "great shift" forward of the Fifth to the Seventeenth or even the last Sunday took place, moving probably the lessons and orations only, while the other parts remained as they had been.

(At dialog and chanted Masses, a hymn may be sung congregationally instead, provided it reflects the same thoughts and emotions as the Psalm or is at least similar in content.)

> Look upon me and have mercy on me, O Lord,
>> For alone and poor am I: see my lowliness and my laboring,
>> And forgive all my sins, O God.

Cong.: And forgive all my sins, O God.

Cantor: To thee do I lift up my soul, O Lord my God:
> In thee do I trust, let me not be put to shame;
> let my enemies not exult over me.

Cong.: And forgive all my sins, O God.

Cantor: Of all who hopefully await thee, not one shall be put to shame;
> Shame waits for those who rashly break faith with thee.

Cong.: And forgive all my sins, O God.

Cantor: Show me, Lord, thy ways, teach me thy paths:
> Guide me in thy truth and teach me,
> For thou art God my Saviour and I await thee all day long.

Cong.: And forgive all my sins, O God.

Cantor: Remember thy pity, Lord, and thy kindness that have been from of old:
> Remember not the sins of my youth and my follies.
> Think of me in thy mercy, because of thy goodness, O Lord.

Cong.: And forgive all my sins, O God.

Cantor: Good is the Lord and just, and so he teaches the afflicted his way.

Cong.: And forgive all my sins, O God.

Unless more of the Psalm must be sung, the choir intones: Glory

---

[2] Psalm 24, is adapted from *Key to the Psalms* by Mary Perkins Ryan (Chicago: Fides, 1956), pp. 142 ff.

be to the Father . . . *And the congregation responds*: As it was in the beginning . . . Amen. *The antiphon is then repeated by the schola or choir.*

4. *In the sanctuary the lower servers group themselves near their own bench, close to the large credence table on the right, after having placed the cross and the candles at the altar. As the celebrant arrives at the altar steps, he bows profoundly (with the two sacred ministers at a solemn Mass, or with the deacon if he alone assists). The deacon (or celebrant) ascends to the altar to deposit the Gospel Book on its mensa, kissing the altar and the book. Then he goes back to the clergy bench, which is located between the credence table and the altar rail.*

The arrival of the celebrant at the altar is the signal for the singing of the Doxology of the Psalm and the final repetition of the Entrance Antiphon.

5. *The Entrance Antiphon completed, the celebrant at the clergy bench sings or says in a loud voice:*

| Kyrie eleison. | Lord have mercy. |

All respond:

| Kyrie eleison. | Lord have mercy. |

Celebrant and congregation alternate through the nine petitions, singing or saying the last one together.

6. *Then the celebrant turns toward the altar and intones:*

Glory be to God on high.

Which is taken up by the choir, alternating the individual verses with the congregation. The conclusion is sung by both.

Choir: And peace on earth to men of good will.

Cong.: We praise thee. We bless thee. We adore thee. We glorify thee.

Choir: We give thee thanks for thy great glory.

Cong.: Lord God, heavenly king, God the Father almighty.

Choir: Lord Jesus Christ, the only-begotten Son,

Cong.: Lord God, Lamb of God, Son of the Father.

Choir: Who takest away the sins of the world, have mercy on us.

Cong.: Who takest away the sins of the world, accept our prayers.

Choir: Who sittest at the right hand of the Father, have mercy on us.

Cong.: For thou alone art holy. Thou alone art Lord.
Choir: Thou alone art the Most High: Jesus Christ with the
Holy Spirit,
All: In the glory of God the Father. Amen.

7. *The celebrant then turns to the congregation and says or sings:*
The Lord be with you.
All: And with your spirit.
Cel.: Let us pray.
All bow their heads in silent prayer.

8. *The Collect is then sung or recited by the celebrant who turns toward*
the altar:
Protector of those who trust in thee, O God,
Without whom nothing is strong, nothing holy:
Increase thy mercy toward us,
Be thou our ruler and guide,
So that we may pass through the good things of this
world
Without losing those of the world to come:
Through our Lord Jesus Christ, thy Son,
Who lives and reigns with thee
In the unity of the Holy Spirit, God,
For ever and ever.
All: Amen.
Thus ends the Entrance Rite of the Mass

The Service of the Word

9. *During the following part of the Mass, all those who are not engaged*
in the actual performance of a reading, etc., are seated, and listen to the
reader. No duplication of readings takes place. While the subdeacon
chants the Epistle, the celebrant listens, and so on. There is no silent or
labial reading of sung or recited texts by anyone (see the rubrics of OHSI
in this matter).

10. *The subdeacon goes to his lectern and reads (a lesson from the Old*
Testament; on this Sunday, perhaps, Isaias 1:15 to 19, followed by the
Gradual now assigned to the Epistle, or, if a second lesson is not con-
templated in the coming reform) the following Epistle (1 Peter 5:6-7)
facing the congregation.

A reading from the Epistle of St. Peter, the Apostle.

Brethren: Bow down before the strong hand of God; he will raise you up, when his time comes to deliver you. Throw back on him the burden of all your anxiety; he is concerned for you. Be sober, and watch well; the devil, who is your enemy, goes about roaring like a lion, to find his prey, but you, grounded in the faith, must face him boldly; you know well enough that the brotherhood you belong to pays, all the world over, the same tribute of suffering. And God, the giver of all grace, who has called us to enjoy, after a little suffering, his eternal glory in Christ Jesus, will himself give you mastery, and steadiness, and strength. To him be glory and power through endless ages. Amen.

The subdeacon or reader returns to the clergy bench and salutes the celebrant who blesses him with a sign of the cross. He sits in his assigned place to listen with the others to the Responsorial Songs.

11. *The Gradual (unless transferred to follow the Lesson) is sung by the choir, by a schola or by the cantor:*

Choir: Cast the burden of thy cares upon the Lord and he will sustain thee.

Cantor: When I called to the Lord, he was not deaf to my appeal for aid against those who attacked me.

Choir: Cast the burden of thy cares upon the Lord and he will sustain thee.

12. *The preparation for the Gospel: the Alleluia (Tract, Sequence, etc.).*

Cantor: Alleluia.

Cong.: Alleluia.

Cantor (or schola): How just a judge is God, how strong, how patient: Would he be angry day by day?

All: Alleluia.

13. *While the preceding is being sung, the deacon goes to the lowest altar step, kneels and says quietly:*

Cleanse my heart and my lips, almighty God, with a live coal as Isaias', that I may be able fitly to announce thy holy Gospel.

Then he brings the Gospel Book from the altar and faces the celebrant to ask his blessing. Making the sign of the cross over him, the celebrant says in a low voice:

The Lord be in thy heart and on thy lips: announce the Gospel worthily.

Preceded by two acolytes with lighted candles and the incense-bearer, the deacon goes to the ambo (pulpit) to sing the Gospel. (In Masses without deacon or subdeacon, the celebrant modifies these ceremonies and omits those parts which are not needed. The Lesson and Epistle are then read by a lector who follows a rite similar to the subdeacon's.)

14. *At the ambo, the deacon (or celebrant) opens the book, incenses it, and, facing the congregation to read the Gospel (Luke 15:1–10), sings or says:*

The Lord be with you.

All: And with your spirit.

Deacon: A passage from the Gospel of Saint Luke.

At this time, when they found all the publicans and sinners coming to listen to Jesus, the Pharisees and scribes were indignant; Here is a man, they said, that entertains sinners, and eats with them. Whereupon he told them this parable: If any of you owns a hundred sheep, and has lost one of them, does he not leave the other ninety-nine in the wilderness, and go after the one which is lost until he finds it? And when he does find it, he sets it on his shoulders, rejoicing, and so goes home, and calls his friends and his neighbors together; Rejoice with me, he says to them, I have found my sheep that was lost. So it is, I tell you, in heaven; there will be more rejoicing over one sinner who repents, than over ninety-nine souls that are justified, and have no need of repentance. Or if some woman has ten silver pieces by her, and has lost one of them, does she not light a lamp, and sweep the house, and search carefully until she finds it? And when she does find it, she calls her friends and her neighbors together; Rejoice with me, she says, I have found the silver piece which I lost. So it is, I tell you, with the angels of God; there is joy among them over one sinner that repents.[3]

15. *The sermon or homily somehow related to the texts read is then delivered. It is to be remembered that it is part of the sacred mysteries, not an interruption.*

16. *Short announcements are then made, mostly referring to the parish bulletin. Letters from the Chancery and appeals should be, if possible, short and pithy. The prayers customary at this point are to be taken up later during the Bidding Prayers.*

[3] Unless the "Praise be to thee, O Christ" is sung solemnly, it would be better to omit it entirely. The "Through the words of the Gospel may our sins be effaced" should be optional, to be said as the celebrant kisses the book.

17. *The Bidding Prayers should be variations on the texts presented above (pp. 56 ff.), according to the season. In our paradigm Mass from the Third Sunday after Pentecost, instead of the pronounced emphasis on the Passion, phrases in accord with the spirit of the season from Pentecost to the Seventeenth Sunday after should be used. The general structure of the Bidding Prayers remains the same, as does the Open Confession. These prayers are led from the ambo by the celebrant or the deacon. The celebrant always pronounces the Absolution and the Collect-like prayer at the end.*

Thus ends the Service of the Word in the Mass

The Offertory Rite

18. *At the clergy bench the celebrant intones:*

I believe in one God

Choir: The Father almighty, maker of heaven and earth,

Cong.: And of all things visible and invisible.

Choir: And in one Lord Jesus Christ, the only-begotten Son of God.

Cong.: Born of the Father before all ages.

Choir: God of God, light of light, true God of true God.

Cong.: Begotten, not made;

Choir: Of one being with the Father: by whom all things were made.

Cong.: Who for us men, and for our salvation came down from heaven.

Choir: And was made flesh by the Holy Spirit, of the Virgin Mary: and was made man.

Cong.: He was also crucified for us,

Choir: Suffered under Pontius Pilate, and was buried.

Cong.: And on the third day He rose again, according to the Scriptures.

Choir: And ascending into heaven, He sits at the right hand of the Father.

Cong.: And He shall come again with glory to judge the living and the dead: and of His kingdom there shall be no end.

Choir: And in the Holy Spirit, the Lord and giver of life,

Cong.: Who proceeds from the Father and the Son.

Choir: Who together with the Father and the Son is adored
and glorified: who spoke by the prophets.

Cong.: And in one, holy, catholic and apostolic Church.

Choir: I confess one baptism for the remission of sins.

Cong.: And I look for the resurrection of the dead.

All: And the life of the world to come. Amen.

19. *While the Creed is being sung by the choir and the congregation,
the sacred ministers vest at the credence table (chasuble, dalmatic, tunic,
and maniples. The celebrant's cope is taken to the sacristy by a server).
The deacon spreads the corporal on the altar mensa and returns to assist
the celebrant. In nonsolemn Masses an acolyte spreads the corporal. The
subdeacon places the Sacramentary (Missal) on the altar in the center,
behind the corporal.*

*At the end of the Creed, the celebrant prepares the gifts at the
credence table. When he uncovers the paten, he says in a low voice:*

Suscipe, sancte pater, sacrificium nostrum quam offerimus pro in-
numerabilibus peccatis et offensionibus et neglegentiis nostris, sed et pro
omnibus vivis atque defunctis ad salutem in vitam aeternam.

When he prepares the chalice, the Celebrant says in the same way:

Offerimus Domine, calicem salutis continentem vinum sanguinem
futurum cuius odor suavis ascendat in conspectu divinae maiestatis tuae.

20. *Then the two offertory processions, accompanied by the singing,
take place. Preceded by the incense bearer, two acolytes with candles
and the assisting subdeacon, the celebrant carries the chalice and paten
to the altar. This ceremony ought to be timed to meet the deacon (acolyte)
in the center of the sanctuary who carries the hosts of the congregation,
which he in turn accepts together with the offerings for the support of
the Church, from the lay representatives at the gate of the sanctuary.
The deacon ascends the altar, and deposits the hosts on the corporal beside the chalice and the offerings on the corner of the altar, on the left
side.*

21. *When the processions are ready to start, the choir intones the Offertory Antiphon, which is then sung either in Latin (plain Chant, polyphony and psalmodic verses) or in English (when permitted), or
substituted for by a suitable and carefully chosen hymn (paraphrasing
the Offertorium, not necessarily expressing ideas of offering — which the
Offertorium seldom does).*

The choir (or soloist) sings the antiphon: [4]

[4] Offertory Antiphon and verses for the Third Sunday after Pentecost
(*Antiphonae Missarum Septuplex*, edited by Dom Hesbert, [Brussels, 1935],
p. 84, 69b).

Sperent in te omnes qui noverunt tuum Domine:

Quoniam non derelinquis quaerentes te.

Psallite Domino qui habitat in Sion:

Quoniam non est oblitus clamorem pauperum.

Cantor:

Sedes super thronum qui iudicas aequitatem:

Increpasti gentes et periit impius.

Iudicare pupillum cum iustitia:

Et factus es refugium pauperum.

All: Et factus est refugium pauperum.

Cantor:

Cognoscetur Dominus iudicia faciens.

Quoniam patientia pauperum non peribit in finem:

Desiderium pauperum exaudivit Deus.

All: Et factus est refugium pauperum.

All hope in thee who know thy name, O Lord,

For thou dost not abandon those who seek thee.

Sing psalms to the Lord who dwells in Sion,

For he has not forgotten the cry of the poor.

Cantor:

Seated on thy throne thou judgest justly:

Thou dost rebuke the heathen, the godless perish.

Judge the little one with justice,

Thou hast made thyself the shelter of the poor.

All: Thou hast made thyself the shelter of the poor.

Cantor:

The Lord will be revealed in passing judgment,

The patience of the poor will not in the end be vain:

God has heard the longing of the poor.

All: Thou hast made thyself the shelter of the poor.

22. *When the gifts have been arranged on the altar, the incensation takes place, performed entirely by the celebrant, who does not leave the footpace of the altar, but freely turns toward the objects of the incensations. He then hands the censer to the deacon to be incensed himself. No prayers are used during the rite of incensation.*

23. *The choir and congregation sing the last unit of the offertory song during the incensation; as soon as they have finished, the celebrant sings or says aloud:*

Oremus.   Let us pray.

86   SAMPLE MASS

After a short pause for silent prayer, the celebrant sings or recites aloud the Oratio super oblata:

> Look down, O Lord, on the gifts of the Church now
> praying to thee:
> And for the salvation of thy faithful.
> Grant that these gifts may be received as an enduring
> sanctification,
> Through our Lord Jesus Christ, thy Son,
> Who lives and reigns with thee in the unity of the
> Holy Spirit,
> For ever and ever.

All: Amen.

Thus end the Offertory Rites of the Mass

Canon Missae

24. *Post moram debitam, celebrans cantat vel dicit clara voce:*
Dominus vobiscum.

Cui omnes respondent:
Et cum spiritu tuo.

Cel.: Sursum corda.

Omnes: Habemus ad Dominum.

Omnes capita inclinant, dum celebrans cantat vel dicit:
Gratias agamus Domino Deo nostro.

Omnes: Dignum et iustum est.

Et celebrans prosequitur: [5]

Vere dignum et iustum est, aequum et salutare,
nos tibi semper et ubique gratias agere,
Domine, sancte Pater, omnipotens aeterne Deus,
per Christum Dominum nostrum:
Cuius hoc mirificum opus ac salutare Mysterium fuit,
ut, perditi dudum atque prostrati a diabolo et mortis
aculeo,
ad hanc gloriam vocaremur qua nunc genus electum,
sacerdotium regale, ac populus acquisitionis et gens
sancta vocemur:
Agentes igitur indefessas gratias, sanctamque munificentiam
tuam praedicantes,
Maiestati tuae haec sacra deferimus, quae nobis salutis nostrae
auctor Christus instituit:
Per quem maiestatem tuam laudent Angeli, adorant Domi-
nationes, tremunt Potestates, Caeli caelorumque Virtutes
ac beata Seraphim socia exsultatione concelebrant:
Cum quibus et nostras voces ut admitti iubeas deprecamur,
supplici confessione dicentes:

Omnes, inclinantes, cantant vel dicunt:

Sanctus, Sanctus, Sanctus, Dominus Deus Sabaoth. Pleni
sunt caeli et terra gloria tua. Hosanna in excelsis.

---

[5] Taken from the *Codex Sangallensis*, 9#348; Mohlberg (Münster, 1939),
2, # 873. Cf. Alban Dold, O.S.B., *Sursum Corda* (Salzburg, 1954). Dom
Alban, in his introduction, expresses the hope that a great number of Prefaces
may be restored to use. This is the Preface he assigns to the Third Sunday
after Pentecost, our model.

The Canon of the Mass

24. *After a suitable pause, the celebrant chants or says in a loud voice:*
> The Lord be with you.

And all reply:
> And with your spirit.

Cel.: Lift up your hearts.

All: We lift them up to the Lord.

All bow their heads, while the celebrant chants or says:
> Let us give thanks to the Lord our God.

All: It is fitting and just.

The celebrant continues:

Indeed it is fitting and just, right and for our salvation,
> that always and everywhere we should give thanks to thee,
> Lord, holy Father, almighty everlasting God,
> through Christ our Lord:

Whose was this wonderful work and saving Mystery —
> that, while we were still lost, brought low by the devil and the sting of death,
> we should have been called to this glory whereby we are now called
> a chosen race, a royal priesthood, a purchased people and a holy nation:

We give thee, then, unwearying thanks and we praise thy divine generosity, as we bring to thy majesty these sacred gifts, instituted for us by Christ, the source of our salvation:

Through whom the Angels praise, the Dominations adore, the Powers worship in trembling, the Heavens, the Powers of heaven and the blessed Seraphim together celebrate thy majesty with joy:

With whom, we pray, command that our voices be admitted also, saying in suppliant praise:

All bow their heads and, with the celebrant, chant or say aloud (with the ringing of bells accompanying):
> Holy, Holy, Holy, Lord God of heavenly Powers. Heaven
and earth are full of thy glory. Hosanna in the highest!

Omnes se erigunt et signant se crucis signo:
Benedictus qui venit in nomine Domini. Hosanna in excelsis.

25. *Et celebrans prosequitur:*

Te igitur, clementissime Pater, per Iesum Christum, Filium tuum, Dominum nostrum, supplices rogamus, ac petimus, uti accepta habeas et bene † dicas, haec dona, haec munera, haec sancta sacrificia illibata: in primis, quae tibi offerimus pro Ecclesia tua sancta catholica: quam pacificare, custodire, adunare et regere digneris toto orbe terrarum: una cum famulo tuo Papa nostro *N.* et Antistite nostro *N.* et omnibus orthodoxis, atque catholicae et apostolicae fidei cultoribus.

26. Memento, Domine, famulorum famularumque tuarum *N.* et *N. Omnes aliquantulum in silentio orant pro quibus orare intendunt;* et omnium circumstantium, quorum tibi fides cognita est, et nota devotio, qui tibi offerunt hoc sacrificium laudis, pro se, suisque omnibus: pro redemptione animarum suarum, pro spe salutis et incolumitatis suae: tibique reddunt vota sua aeterno Deo, vivo et vero.

Communicantes, et memoriam venerantes, in primis gloriosae semper Virginis Mariae, Genitricis Dei et Domini nostri Iesu Christi: sed et beatorum Apostolorum ac Martyrum tuorum, Petri et Pauli, et omnium sanctorum tuorum: quorum meritis precibusque concedas, ut in omnibus protectionis tuae muniamur auxilio.

27. *Tenens manus expansas super oblata, celebrans dicit:*

Hanc igitur oblationem servitutis nostrae, sed et cunctae familiae tuae, quaesumus, Domine, ut placatus accipias: diesque nostros in tua pace disponas, atque ab aeterna damnatione nos eripi, et in electorum tuorum iubeas grege numerari.

28. Quam oblationem tu, Deus, in omnibus, quaesumus, bene † dictam, adscriptam, ratam, rationabilem, acceptabilemque facere digneris: ut nobis Corpus, et Sanguis fiat dilectissimi Filii tui, Domini nostri Iesu Christi.

All stand erect and make the sign of the cross:

Blessed is he who comes in the name of the Lord. Hosanna in the highest!

25. *And the celebrant continues:*

O Father most merciful, we humbly pray thee through Jesus Christ thy son our Lord, and we ask thee to welcome and to bless these gifts, these presents, these holy unspoiled sacrifices. First and foremost for thy holy catholic Church do we offer them to thee — be pleased to grant her throughout the entire world tranquillity, protection, unity and peace. We offer them too for thy servant *N.* our Pope and for *N.* our Bishop and for all the faithful guardians of the catholic and apostolic faith.

26. Remember, O Lord, thy servants and thy handmaids *N.* and *N. All pray silently for a little while for those for whom they intend to pray;* and all those here around us, for thou knowest their faith, their loyalty, who offer thee this sacrifice of praise for themselves and for all their kith and kin, to obtain redemption for their souls, the salvation they hope for, and freedom from all danger; and they address their prayers to thee, the eternal, the living and the true God.

United in one communion, we venerate in the first place the memory of the glorious Mary ever Virgin, Mother of our God and Lord Jesus Christ; and the memory too of thy blessed Apostles Peter and Paul and of all thy saints. Moved by their merits and their prayers, grant us thy help and thy protection in all circumstances.

27. *The celebrant then stretches his hands over the gifts saying:*

Accept then, O Lord with favor and indulgence this offering from us thy servants and from thy whole family too; dispose our days in thy peace; preserve us from eternal damnation, and number us within the fold of thy elect.

28. Do Thou, O Lord, deign to make this offering in every way a bles † sed offering, an accepted offering, an approved offering; deign to make it a perfect and worthy offering, so that it may become for us the Body and the Blood of thy well-beloved Son, our Lord Jesus Christ.

29. Qui pridie quam pateretur, *celebrans accipit hostiam*, accepit panem in sanctas ac venerabiles manus suas, et elevatis oculis in caelum ad te Deum Patrem suum omnipotentem, tibi gratias agens, bene † dixit, fregit, deditque discipulis suis, dicens: Accipite, et manducate ex hoc omnes.

Hoc est enim Corpus meum.

30. *Et ambabus manibus accipiens calicem, celebrans prosequitur:*

Simili modo postquam coenatum est, accipiens et hunc praeclarum Calicem in sanctas ac venerabiles manus suas: item tibi gratias agens, bene † dixit, deditque discipulis suis, dicens: Accipite, et bibite ex eo omnes.

Hic est enim Calix Sanguinis mei, novi et aeterni testamenti: mysterium fidei: qui pro vobis and pro multis effundetur in remissionem peccatorum.

Haec quotiescumque feceritis, in mei memoriam facietis.

31. Unde et memores, Domine, nos servi tui, sed et plebs tua sancta, eiusdem Christi Filii tui Domini nostri tam beatae passionis, nec non et ab inferis resurrectionis, sed et in caelos gloriosae ascensionis: offerimus praeclarae maiestati tuae de tuis donis ac datis, hostiam puram, hostiam sanctam, hostiam immaculatam, Panem sanctum vitae aeternae, et Calicem salutis perpetuae.

32. Supra quae propitio ac sereno vultu respicere digneris: et accepta habere, sicuti accepta habere dignatus es munera pueri tui iusti Abel, et sacrificium Patriarchae nostri Abrahae: et quod tibi obtulit summus sacerdos tuus Melchisedech, sanctum sacrificium, immaculatam hostiam.

33. Supplices te rogamus, omnipotens Deus: iube haec perferri per manus sancti Angeli tui in sublime altare tuum, in conspectu divinae maiestatis tuae: ut quotquot ex hac altaris participatione sacrosanctum Filii tui Corpus, et Sanguinem sumpserimus, omni benedictione caelesti et gratia repleamur.

(Short bell signal to indicate the beginning of the Consecration.)

29. He, on the eve of his passion, took bread into his holy, his majestic hands, *the celebrant takes up the host,* and with eyes raised up towards heaven to thee, O God, his Father Almighty, offering thanks to thee, he bless † ed, broke and gave it to his disciples, saying: Take, all of you, and eat of this.

For this is my Body.

30. *And taking up the chalice with both hands, the celebrant continues:*

In like manner after the Supper, taking in turn this noble chalice into his holy, his majestic hands, in the same way offering thanks to thee, he blessed it and gave it to his disciples saying: Take, all of you, and drink of this.

For this is the chalice of my Blood, of the new and eternal testament, the mystery of faith, which shall be shed for you and for many for the remission of sins.

As often as you shall do these things, you shall do them in memory of me.

(Short bell signal to indicate the end of the Consecration).

31. In memory, then, O Lord of the most blessed passion of this same Christ thy Son, our Lord, and of his resurrection from the dead, as well as of his ascension into the glory of heaven, we thy servants and thy holy people too, offer to thy august majesty — out of thy own gifts and bounties — the pure victim, the holy victim, the immaculate victim, the holy Bread of eternal life, and the Chalice of everlasting salvation.

32. Deign to look down on them with kindly and tranquil favor, and to accept them as thou didst accept the gifts of thy servant Abel the Just and the sacrifice of our Patriarch Abraham, and that which Melchisedech thy high priest offered thee, a holy sacrifice, an immaculate victim.

33. We, thy suppliants, O almighty God, beg thee to have these offerings brought to thy altar on high by the hands of thy holy angel, in sight of thy divine majesty, so that we who shall receive at this partaking of the altar the most sacred Body and Blood of thy Son, may all be filled with every heavenly blessing and grace.

34. Memento etiam, Domine, famulorum famularumque tuarum *N.* et *N.*, qui nos praecesserunt cum signo fidei, et dormiunt in somno pacis. *Omnes aliquantulum in silentio orant pro quibus orare intendunt.* Ipsis, Domine et omnibus in Christo quiescentibus, locum refrigerii, lucis et pacis, ut indulgeas, deprecamur.

35. *Celebrans inclinato aliquantulum capite pectus percutit dicens clara voce:*

Nobis quoque peccatoribus, famulis tuis, de multitudine miserationum tuarum sperantibus, partem aliquam et societatem donare digneris, cum tuis sanctis Apostolis et Martyribus : cum Ioanne, Stephano et omnibus Sanctis tuis : intra quorum nos consortium, non aestimator meriti, sed veniae, quaesumus, largitor admitte. Per Christum Dominum nostrum : per quem haec omnia, Domine, semper bona creas, sanctificas, vivificas, benedicis et praestas nobis :

36. *Celebrans accipit hostiam et calicem et tenet ea elevata ad Deum, in conspectu populi, dum cantat vel clara voce dicit:*

Per ipsum, et cum ipso, et in ipso, est tibi Deo Patri omnipotenti, in unitate Spiritus Sancti, omnis honor et gloria, per omnia saecula saeculorum.

Et omnes respondent:

37. Amen.

Explicit canon Missae

34. Remember also, O Lord, thy servants and thy handmaids *N.* and *N.*, who have gone before us sealed with the seal of faith, and who sleep the sleep of peace. *All pray silently for a little while for those for whom they intend to pray*; To them, O Lord, and to all who rest in Christ, grant, we beseech thee, the abode of consolation, of light and of peace.

35. *The celebrant makes a slight bow of the head and strikes his breast at the words:*

We sinners too place our hope in the profusion of thy mercies; deign to grant us some part and fellowship with thy holy Apostles and Martyrs: with John, Stephen, and with all thy Saints. Admit us, we pray, to their company, not questioning our merits but lavishing thy pardon. Through Christ our Lord, through whom, O Lord, thou dost ever create and sanctify, endow with life and bless all these good things and givest them to us:

36. *The celebrant takes the host and chalice into his hands, elevates them to God for all to see, while he sings or says in a loud voice:*

Through him, and with him, and in him, is to thee, O God the Father almighty, in the unity of the Holy Spirit, all honor, all glory, world without end.

And all answer:

37. Amen.

Thus ends the Canon of the Mass

Communion Rite

38. The celebrant, having observed a noticeable pause of silence after the solemn Amen, sings or recites with a loud voice:

Let us pray: Obeying our Saviour's command and taught by his divine institution, we dare to say:

39. All joining their voices to that of the celebrant, sing or say:

Our Father, who art in heaven,
Hallowed be Thy Name.
Thy Kingdom come.
Thy will be done, on earth as it is in heaven.
Give us this day our daily Bread.
And forgive us our trespasses,
As we forgive them that trespass against us,
And lead us not into temptation,
But deliver us from evil.

40. The celebrant then continues alone in a loud voice, without any accompanying rite:

Deliver us, we pray thee, O Lord, from all evils, past, present and to come. And by the intercession of the blessed and glorious Mary, ever a Virgin, with thy holy Apostles Peter and Paul, and Andrew, and all the saints, in thy kindness grant peace in our days, so that, sustained by the work of thy mercy, we may be always free from sin and secure from all disturbance: through Jesus Christ, thy Son, our Lord, who lives and reigns with thee in the unity of the Holy Spirit, God, for ever and ever.

All: Amen.

41. The celebrant continues silently:

Lord Jesus Christ, who didst say to thine Apostles: Peace I leave to you, my peace I give you: look not upon my sins, but upon the faith of thy Church: be pleased, according to thy will, to give her peace and to gather her together in unity, O God who livest and reignest for ever and ever. Amen.

The celebrant sings:

The peace of the Lord be always with you.

42. Several small crosses or pax tablets (Pax-brede) are ready on the credence table; after the celebrant has given the Kiss of Peace to the assistants in the sanctuary, the deacon (or an acolyte in the absence of a deacon) holds the tablets in front of the celebrant who blesses them with

*a sign of the cross, then carries them to the altar gate and distributes
them to the ushers, saying to each of them:*

Peace be with you.

Recipient: And with you.

*The pax tablets are then carried from pew to pew and passed among the
faithful in the same manner.*

43. *When the deacon returns to the side of the celebrant, the choir (or
cantor or lector) sings or says:*

Lamb of God, who takest away the sins of the world:

All: Have mercy on us.

This is repeated three times, but the third time the response is:

Grant us peace.

*While the Agnus Dei is being chanted the celebrant breaks his Host
into three parts; one for his own Communion, one for the deacon and
one for the subdeacon. If no subdeacon is present the third part is given
to the acolytes. The same is done at sung Mass and recited Mass.*

44. *Meanwhile the celebrant may say in silence and privately the following prayers, unless he prefers to pray in his own words:*

Lord Jesus Christ, Son of the living God, who, by the Father's will
and the cooperation of the Holy Spirit, didst by thy death bring life to
the world, deliver me by this most holy Body and Blood of thine from all
my sins and from every evil. Make me always cling to thy command-
ments, and never allow me to be parted from thee: who with the self-
same God the Father and the Holy Spirit art God, living and reigning for
ever and ever. Amen.

Let not the partaking of thy Body, Lord Jesus Christ, which I, un-
worthy as I am, make bold to receive, turn against me into judgment and
damnation, but through thy loving-kindness let it be for me a safeguard
of mind and body, and in it let me find healing: thou who art God, living
and reigning with God the Father in the unity of the Holy Spirit, world
without end. Amen.

I will take the Bread of Heaven, and will call upon the name of the
Lord.

Lord, I am not worthy that thou shouldst come under my roof, but
only say the word, and my soul will be healed (*no bell*).

The Body of our Lord Jesus Christ preserve my soul for everlasting
life. Amen.

The Blood of our Lord Jesus Christ preserve my soul for life everlasting. Amen.

45. *After communicating himself the celebrant gives Holy Communion
to the deacon and the subdeacon without further introductory prayers,
as also to the servers in the sanctuary on the footpace of the altar.*

46. *Then the celebrant takes the ciborium into his hand and raises one Host with his right hand for all to see and says aloud:*

Behold the Lamb of God, behold him who takes away the sins of the world.

All then say (three times) in unison in a loud voice:

Lord, I am not worthy that thou shouldst come under my roof, but only say the word and my soul shall be healed.

47. *After the last words have been said the choir intones the Processional for Communion (Luke 15:10):*

> I say unto you: there is joy among the angels of God over one sinner who repents.

All: Over one repentant sinner there is joy.

Cantor: To thee do I lift up my soul, Lord my God: In thee do I trust, let me not be put to shame, let my enemies not exult over me.

All: Over one repentant sinner there is joy.

Cantor: Of all who hopefully await thee, not one shall be put to shame; shame waits for those who rashly break faith with thee.

All: Over one repentant sinner there is joy.

Cantor: Show me, Lord, thy ways, teach me thy paths: Guide me in thy truth and teach me, For thou art God my Saviour and I await thee all day long.

All: Over one repentant sinner there is joy.

Cantor: Remember thy pity, Lord, and thy kindness that have been from of old: Remember not the sins of my youth and my follies. Think of me in thy mercy, because of thy goodness, O Lord.

All: Over one repentant sinner there is joy.

Unless more of the Psalm must be sung, the choir intones: Glory be to the Father. . . . *And the congregation responds*: As it was in the beginning . . . Amen.

The Antiphon is then repeated by the schola or choir.

48. *When the choir starts the processional, the celebrant (and the deacon) take Communion to the faithful, both distributing the holy Sacra-*

ment. *If there is a great crowd and time is short, other priests and deacons should help and in this case take ciboria out of the tabernacle. All ciboria are taken back to the tabernacle after the congregation has been served. To expedite the distribution, the ushers should see that the people form several processional columns, well-distributed along the altar rail. When there is a large crowd, the faithful should file by the stationary priests and deacons, receiving standing up and making a genuflection before Communion only.*

To every communicant the ministering priest or deacon says:[6]

The Body of Christ!

The communicant responds: Amen

49. *After returning to the altar, the celebrant and deacon purify the paten and chalice and cover them in the traditional way. They may accompany the action with the following silent prayers:*

That which our mouths have taken, Lord, may we possess in purity of heart; and may the gift of the moment become for us an everlasting remedy.

May thy Body, Lord, which I have taken, and thy Blood which I have drunk, cleave to every fiber of my being. Grant that no stain of sin may be left in me, now that I am renewed by this pure and holy sacrament; who livest and reignest world without end. Amen.

50. *The deacon (or celebrant) carries the chalice to the credence table and both take their places at the bench, the celebrant turns to the congregation and sings or says:*

The Lord be with you.

All: And with your spirit.

Cel.: Let us pray.

After a noticeable pause for private prayer with heads bowed, the celebrant sings or says:

O Lord, may thy holy gifts which we have received give us life, and may they prepare us, thus cleansed, for everlasting mercy, through our Lord, Jesus Christ, thy Son who lives and reigns with thee, God the Father in the unity of the Holy Spirit, God, for ever and ever.

All: Amen

51. *The celebrant then sings:*

The Lord be with you.

All: And with your spirit.

[6] Or: The Body of our Lord Jesus Christ!

Deacon (or celebrant): Go, the Mass is completed.

All: Praise to God.

52. *The celebrant goes to the altar, while the procession of the assistants is formed. He kisses the altar as a farewell, and then imparts the Blessing to the congregation before they depart:*

May God almighty bless you: the Father and the Son and the Holy Spirit.

All: Amen.

53. *The procession moves on the shorter way to the sacristy, while a recessional is sung: a hymn, a Marian antiphon, the Laudes Hincmari or an organ postlude.*

Postscript

After finishing the manuscript of this small book, I described its plan and purpose to a friend of mine, a rabbi. He listened very attentively, and then said: "A very neat plan indeed — too neat for me. We Jews reformed our rites a hundred years ago; we cut off what was wild growth, as we saw it, and we introduced the 'colloquial' — which means more than a 'vernacular' — language. But we have learned that we made a mistake: we lost the sacredness and the mystery of our rites. Now all is obvious and trite; the beauty is gone."

Many people besides my rabbi friend may have the same fears; but are these in any way justified? I really do not think there is any resemblance between the two cases: this past reform of the rites of the synagogue and the projected reform of the Mass. The Mass has a basic plan, an essential structure which may unfold in various ways; the reform is being planned with a deep respect for tradition, a vast store of historical data and, above all, the supervision of the Apostolic See.

Do the outlines given in this work indicate any loss of the constituents of the psychological category of the "sacred," that complex of what Rudolf Otto thirty years ago analyzed as the *mysterium tremendum, fascinosum, numinosum,* that is, the awe and fear, the irresistible attraction and the response to the infinite power of the Almighty? Does trembling fascination before the numinous really represent all our reactions in the face of the Mystery of the Mass? A Platonic and Gnostic sense

101

of awe, as we find it in the writings of Pseudo-Dionysius and in much of the Byzantine liturgy, may heighten an Old-Testament fear and awe like that of the prophets; these elements are certainly present in such prayers as the Preface-Sanctus in our liturgy.

But the Mass is, above all, the Lord's Supper, the Memorial of His humanity as well as of His divinity. The Mystery should not be sought in rites for their own sake, in an almost-folklorish preservation of historical debris, collected by the ebb and flow of the liturgical stream as it coursed through the centuries. The Mystery should be sought where it really is: in the symbols chosen by the Master — bread and wine, combined with His word. It does not consist in the use of a foreign tongue, however ancient and sonorous that tongue may be, nor in the remnant of a rite which has become as incomprehensible as that with the empty paten, as misleading as that of immixtion or as foreign to the Roman spirit as the two trinitarian prayers.

The proposed changes clarify the essential structure of the Mass, so that each stage develops out of its predecessor. There is no longer the danger of becoming confused by now-meaningless rites. The changes will make the Mass more comprehensible (especially in the Communion rite) to the parish priest and his congregation. They do not attempt to popularize or colloquialize the Mass and thus lead to anarchy and formlessness. These changes are in the great liturgical tradition, going back to the best sources.

As the Mass becomes more lucid and as the wild growth is cut away, the Mass is most assuredly not stripped of its mystery; rather the mystery is reemphasized and pin-pointed, as it were. Our sense of mystery is directed to the Mystery par excellence: the proclamation of God's word, the making present of Christ's redemption and that mysterious communal meal which unites the Christian with Christ and welds Christian to Christian in the Body of Christ which is the Church. This is the place to see the mystery, not in quaint and precious rites that leave the expert mystified and the *mystes* puzzled and despairing. Not all that is, is the best that might be; and the Church must have the right to "have pity on the flock."

The reform now under way is superior to preceding ones both in knowledge and motive. As to knowledge: the research of the last decades has put us in a position better than that enjoyed by our predecessors for understanding the essential structure of the Mass and the development of the various rites. As to motive: the purpose of the reform of Charlemagne and Alcuin was uniformity, discipline, and the personal devotion of the clergy; the purpose of that of Trent was simply to put an end to confusion. But Pius XII, following St. Pius X, wanted to enable the spiritually underfed and thirsting masses to refresh themselves at the "primary and indispensible source of the true Christian spirit," and to make the Sacrament a matter of true prayer, to which a feeling of wonderment is only a preliminary step.

Appendix A

A resume of the resolutions of the liturgical congresses at Maria Laach (1951), Ste Odile (1952) and Lugano (1953).

This résumé is taken from the official report on the Third Liturgical Congress, held from September 15 to 18 in 1953, that was prepared by Luigi Agustoni and Johannes Wagner (published at Lugano by the Centro di Liturgia Pastorale) which sums up the two preceding congresses, incorporating the main resolutions taken at these meetings.

The first seventeen of these proposals had already been mentioned at the Maria Laach meeting two years previously.

1. Abolition of present duplication of readings.

2. Omission of the Judica, etc.

3. The second part of the Mass should be called: the Liturgy of the Word. It should be carried out *in choro*, not at the altar.

4. Never more than *one* Collect (with rare exceptions).

5. A three- or four-year *cycle of Lessons* and *Gospels* for Sundays.

6. Less frequent recitation of the Credo.

7. The *Prex fidelium* (Bidding Prayers) — should be reintroduced as the conclusion of the Liturgy of the Word. Omit the Dominus vobiscum at the beginning of the Offertory.

8. The sacred vessels should not be on the altar before the Offertory.

9. More Prefaces, but only those which refer to the *Memoria Passionis*.

104

10. The priest should wait for the end of the Sanctus to continue the Mass. The different Amens during the Canon should be eliminated.

11. No Confiteor, etc., at Communion time.

12. No last Gospel. The Last Blessing ends the Mass.

13. Rename the *Secreta*: "Oratio super oblata," and make it the audible conclusion of the Offertory.

14. Sing the Great Doxology at the end of the Canon; eliminate its five signs of the cross and elevate the two Sacred Species during the Doxology. No genuflection before this elevation and perhaps no genuflection at all.

15. After the Pater noster: regroup the prayers and ceremonies and find a way to have the congregation participate in the Pax.

16. Develop the interval between Communion and Postcommunion (prayers and singing, consult other liturgies).

17. Regulate the use of Ite missa est and Benedicamus Domino (see the new regulation on Holy Thursday).

Proposals 18–26 had already been mentioned at the Conference at Ste Odile.

18. The revised Easter Vigil is the model of the principles which should govern future reforms.

19. Sing or recite aloud the Per ipsum (Great Doxology); no signs of the cross; elevate the two Species until the Amen of the people; no genuflection here, or only after the Amen [repeating no. 14].

20. No Amen after the Pater noster; sing or recite aloud the Libera nos; no sign of the cross with the empty paten, no kiss [anticipating projects of Lugano].

21. Place the first Domine Jesu Christe immediately after the Libera (or suppress it entirely); follow with Pax Domini sit semper vobiscum with no ceremony of the Host; no response of the people; give Pax afterward (this is spelled out in detail on pp. 242–3 of the report).

22. Breaking of the Host takes place after the Pax, with no accompanying ceremony, while the congregation sings the

Agnus Dei; at low Mass the priest says it after the Fractio. The two Communion prayers should then follow or be suppressed (see pp. 242–4 of the report).

23. The celebrant receives half the Host, the other half is either given to those who serve at the altar or distributed with the ciborium.

24. No Confiteor, etc., at Communion time; shortening of the "Corpus" prayer during the distribution (p. 239 of the report elaborates the 1951 Maria Laach resolution).

25. Have the Communio sung solemnly during the distribution, even in the vernacular.

26. At the end of the Mass: Ite missa est (only), Deo gratias, kiss of the altar (no Placeat), blessing, and people's Amen. No Last Gospel or Leonine prayers.

These resolutions were proposed to the Sacred Congregation of Rites, and are the basis of most of the suggestions made in this book. We ask the readers to keep in mind, especially when this book seems to be bold or radical, that the company we are keeping consists of the cream of liturgical scholars.

Appendix B

Righting the Imbalance Between the Offertory and Canon

The Offertory grew to such proportions that in the late Middle Ages it became known as the Little Canon. Not only the amount, but also the content of its prayers are out of all proportion to the significance of the rite in the whole Mass. Compared with the proscomidy of the Eastern rite, it is of course a sober Roman affair. But at about the same time as the proscomidy with its manifold sacrificial rites was introduced in the East, the West introduced the long and complicated Offertory that we have today and imbued it with the spirit of sacrifice — in addition to the Sacrifice of the Mass properly speaking which takes place through the Consecration and the Canon.

The priest lifts the host on his paten, making the following offering:

> Accept, O holy Father, almighty and eternal God, this spotless host, which I, thy unworthy servant offer unto thee, my living and true God, to atone for my numberless sins, offenses and negligences; on behalf of all here present and likewise for all faithful Christians living and dead, that it may profit me and them as a means of salvation unto life everlasting. Amen.

Then he steps over to the epistle side of the altar, fills the chalice with wine and pours in water saying a prayer which refers to the "mystery of this wine and water," thus indicating that this is a rite of significance and reality, symbolizing the union of the divine and the human natures in Christ. Compared with the Greek rite and also with the Commixtio after the Pater noster, this is a mild form of ritual excrescence, but still it is a rite that is not a true dogmatic or historical development according to the essential lines of the Mass.

Returning to the middle of the altar, the priest then offers the chalice with the following prayer:

> We offer unto thee, O Lord, the chalice of salvation, humbly begging of thy mercy that it may arise before thy divine majesty with a pleasing fragrance, for our salvation and that of all the world. Amen.
>
> In a humble spirit and a contrite heart, may we be accepted by thee, O Lord, and may our sacrifice so be offered in thy sight this day as to please thee, O Lord God.

Then follows a blessing addressed obviously to the Holy Spirit who is asked to descend on the gifts on the altar in a "pre-epicletic" benediction.

> Come, thou Sanctifier, almighty and eternal God, and bless this Sacrifice prepared for the glory of thy holy name.

After the washing of the hands (and the incensation of the altar at high Mass), the priest comes back to the middle of the altar and offers another very long prayer, including a whole anamnesis, asking the Blessed Trinity to accept the sacrifice, thus anticipating the prayer that is offered up after the Consecration.

These are weighty words and weighty intentions. The surface meaning of all this prayer is that there is a real sacrifice at this point in the Mass — and this is, obviously, strictly proleptic. Without entering into the historical development of our present Offertory and making a point out of the time when it was introduced, it is obvious that this is an attempt to locate the sacrifice of the Mass somewhere in the Mass. Why was this thought to be necessary?

There may have been many reasons why this amplification of the sacrificial aspect was emphasized in the Offertory, but I am quite sure that one of them was the fact that the *sacrificial aspect of the Canon had become lost* in the silence and in the double elevation. (This tendency is paralleled in the Greek liturgy of Byzantium which also concentrates on the fact of transubstantiation by keeping complete silence between the beginning of the Preface and the singing aloud of the words of consecration and epiclesis.) If we examine the prayers of the Canon, we find that they are, in fact, full of subtle references to the Sacrifice of Christ. If the Canon had continued to be read aloud or sung, the whole community of the faithful would have heard these references: the Body and Blood consecrated separately, the sacrificial intentions of Christ, the anamnesis, and especially the prayers after the anamnesis which speak of the sacrifice of Melchisedech, of Abel, of Abraham and the heavenly sacrifice on high.

Let us imagine for a moment the form and shape of the Canon before these changes took place. It was opened by what now call the Preface, followed by the Sanctus (after the latter was introduced). Then followed the Te igitur, the reading of the diptichs, the Communicantes, and then the Hanc igitur — all this aloud leading up to the pronunciation of the words of consecration. These were followed by the loud sung anamnesis, the reference to the sacrifices of Abel, Abraham and Melchisedech, and the plea that this sacrifice be borne on high by the angel, followed by the diptichs for the dead, and ending with the Great Doxology, accompanying the showing of the Host and Chalice in a solemn elevation, concluded by the Amen of the congregation.

It is obvious to me that nobody could come away from hearing this series of prayers without feeling that the mystery of Christ's sacrifice, of Christ's whole work of redemption had been performed. When in the later Middle Ages, all this was carried out in silence, and the emphasis was put on the fact of the Real Presence by the institution of the two elevations at the

Consecration, the vision of sacrifice and sacrificial action was lost to view. People felt that they were present at the silent making present of the Body of Christ, especially when, due to theological speculations about the Sacrament, the emphasis was put not so much on the real presence of what is there through the power of the words of consecration, but on the presence of what is there by *implication,* by concomitance.

It was quite natural, therefore, that efforts should have been made to preserve the spirit of the Sacrifice of the Mass and to give special emphasis to its sacrificial character. For example, there were the allegorical efforts of Amalar to interpret the whole Mass as a re-presentation of the redemptive work of Christ, to see in every move that was made some phase of this redemptive work. As abstruse as this effort was and as futile as it proved to be, it was a serious attempt to preserve the fullness of the mystery of redemption in the minds of the spectators. And it is not astonishing that these efforts at allegory were made after the Canon had been silenced. But since allegories always lead to arbitrary interpretations and one author did not agree with the other, and since other developments took place that narrowed the allegorism to the one phase of Christ's death, new outlets were sought and found. In the Greek liturgy, the proscomidy included bearing to the altar the gifts *to be* consecrated as solemnly as if they had *already been* consecrated. In Western liturgy, with its greater sobriety and less effort at being dramatic, the Offertory was given greater significance. What was still only bread and wine was declared, long before the Consecration, to be "intentionally" the Body and Blood of our Lord Jesus Christ and thus the Offertory assumed the form of a "Little Canon." This is one of the reasons why, in all modern efforts to reform the Mass, the Little Canon is stripped of its anticipatory character, and has been made into a simple preparation of the gifts and of the minds of the people and the priest.

It seems obvious that the existing imbalance between the really far less significant rite of preparation and the far more significant and important Canon needs to be righted. And this would seem to be one more reason why the Canon should be once again sung aloud or recited in a loud voice and why the elevations should be moved back to the end of the Canon. This would help to restore the proper balance between the Offertory and the Canon, for what is more important and essential to the Mass would be in its right place and given its full emphasis. This would also restore the right balance between the Sacrifice and the Banquet because, as things are, the symbolic actions carry little notion of sacrifice. On the surface everything points to a banquet — bread and wine, the invitation to eat and to drink, and the final consumption of the Holy Species either by the priest alone or by the congregation also. The sacrifice is brought out by the separate consecration of the bread and wine, by the words and hints in the text, and the direct references to the sacrifices of the Old Testament. By saying or singing the Canon aloud, and by carrying out the solemn separate elevations of the Host and Chalice at the moment of the Great Doxology, not only would the balance between Canon and Offertory be restored, but also the balance between the aspect of the sacrifice and that of the banquet.

Much of the effectiveness of the future reform of the Mass will depend on the correct balancing of the various aspects and parts of the whole rite, and on the pastoral emphasis given to them. The restoration of the right proportions will lead to a truer appreciation of what the Mass is, to better individual participation in the Mass, to fuller and more fruitful congregational participation, leading to more total Christian living by aware and active members of the Mystical Body of Christ.

Appendix C

The Texts Used in the Sample Mass

The Latin Text is that of the present Roman Missal, except for the new Psalter. After the late Father John P. O'Connell's article in the *Catholic Biblical Quarterly* (1958, pp. 63 ff), it became clear to me that our assumption that the 1570 *Missale Romanum* was built up of snippets from the Vulgate was an error, and one shared by most missal-makers; but since only two or three lessons are involved in my paradigm Mass this is not too important for us. The reader will therefore find:

The Ordinary and Proper of the Mass are from the existing Roman Missal (except for the omissions of the various extra "conclusions" etc., in the Canon as described in Chapter 3; pp. 64–67), with the new Psalter used where needed and the spelling of the OHSI ("I" for "J"). To replace the "antiphonal" parts of the Latin Mass by the revised Psalter would be a serious mistake and not in the tradition of the several previous reforms, for the antiphonal parts (Introit antiphon, Gradual, Tract, Offertory, and Communion processional antiphon) go back to Latin versions which precede even St. Jerome's several revisions. They should therefore not be judged by their fidelity to a critical version close to the original, but rather be regarded as free and apt paraphrases of biblical texts. This does not mean that they were not once regarded as faithful biblical quotations. Unless they are all recast in the new Missal — which is quite possible — they are the only standard we have. We are on good ground here. When in the fourth century the "Gallican" Psalter superseded the so-called "Roman" Psalter, and again when in 1943 the latest Latin version was made under our late pontiff, the antiphonal texts, because they are highly allusive and fraught with their own musical and symbolic connotations, were left untouched. There is, therefore, a practical reason as well as a theoretical one for leaving these texts alone. An example may illustrate this: no one has so far tried to change the "Apostle Introit" ("Mihi autem nimis honorati sunt amici tui, Deus") although it is not a correct version of what Psalm 137 says. This antiphon, like several others, has become a set liturgical formula: it may be dropped, it may be replaced, but to correct it would be murder. Does the new rendering of the same passage, "Mihi autem quam ardua sunt consilia tua, Deus," have the slightest resemblance to an Introit antiphon for any apostle? It is obvious that reforming zeal finds its limits, unless we are to make a new liturgy and abandon the old.

I may say that some of my sources have suggested a "start from scratch," using the existing liturgy as a pattern only and clothing its bare bones with new flesh. If we did that we should also lose the chant, and it is hardly likely that this will be done. After all, St. Pius X started with a reform of the chant, and by restoring or renewing a chant based on the best available tradition, he created a pattern for the future. Among the abundance of source material found in chant manuscripts, the monks of Solesme who were entrusted with the work of reconstruction had to make choices. If they had followed the ironclad rule of always selecting either the most ancient source or the version of the majority of sources, the results would have been chaotic. I don't feel competent to go into a detailed discussion of this matter, except to say that here too theory and practice together have produced an acceptable and creditable result.

The English Text. For the New Testament lessons, I have used the Knox translation (© Sheed & Ward, 1950) for reasons of readability and faithfulness to the original, having in mind that this selection has little bearing on the official selection which will have to be made by the proper authorities. Most other versions are either avowedly preliminary or private undertakings just as the Knox.

The translation of the Canon is based on the work of Dom Placid Murray, O.S.B., which was published in *The Furrow* in October of 1955 (Maynooth: Saint Patrick's College); which translation in turn is based on the great research work in ecclesiastical and liturgical Latin carried out by such scholars as B. Botte, C. Mohrmann, Battifol, Jungmann, Capelle, etc., and is vastly superior to that of most Missals in catching the overtones of the period of Latinity in which the Roman canon was originally cast. For example, one Missal has come close to translating *cultores fidei* as "practicing Catholics"; the phrase really means those who "cultivate" (like farmers) the faith.

The translation of the rest of the Mass I did myself with an eye on such authorities as Mohrmann, Botte, Murray, Casel, O'Connell-Finberg and other versions. I don't flatter myself by assuming that I have produced the synthesis of all these great and learned efforts, but, if the result is a better understanding of the ecclesiastical and liturgical overtones of the missal-Latin, so much the better.